Street Atlas of
STOKE-ON-TRENT and District

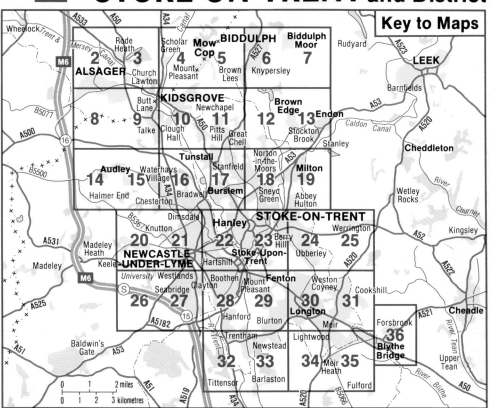

Key to Maps

Reference

Geographers' A-Z Map Co., Ltd.

Head Office: Fairfield Road, Borough Green, Sevenoaks, Kent. TN15 8PP   Telephone 0732 781000
Showrooms: 44 Gray's Inn Road, Holborn, London WC1X 8LR   Telephone 071-242-9246
The Maps in this Atlas are based upon the Ordnance Survey 1:10000 Maps with the permission of the Controller of Her Majesty's Stationery Office.   © Crown Copyright

© 1992   Edition 2   Copyright of the Publishers

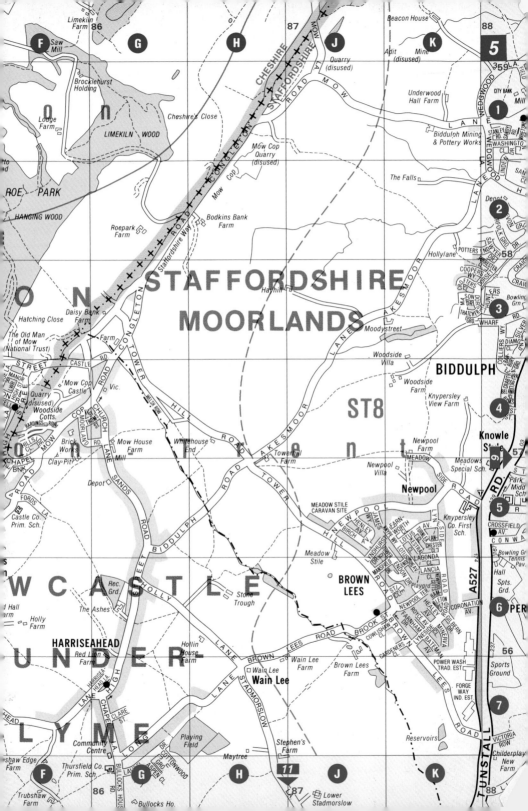

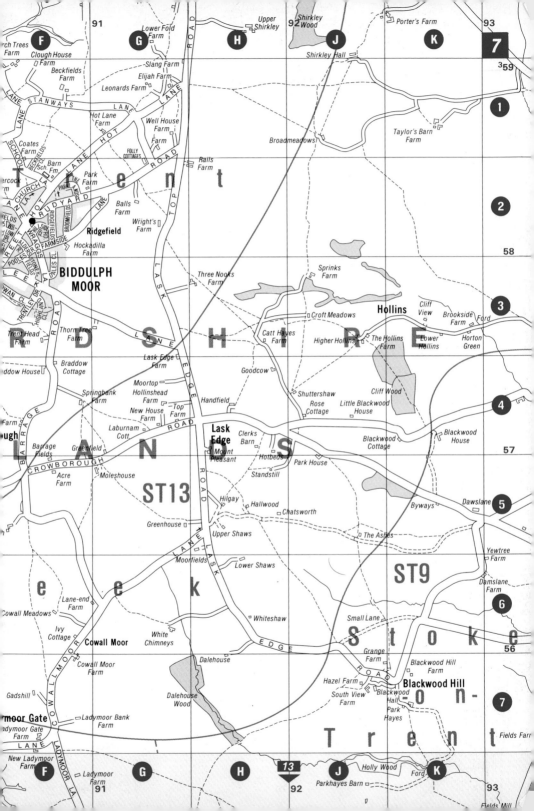

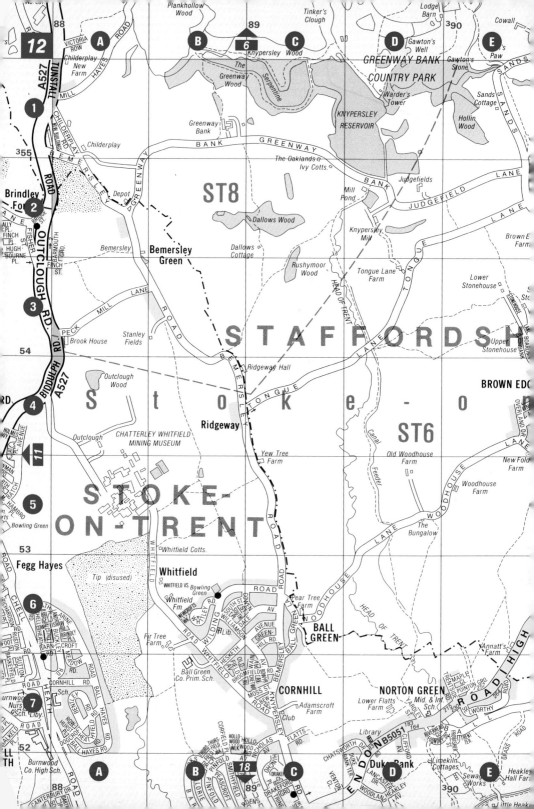

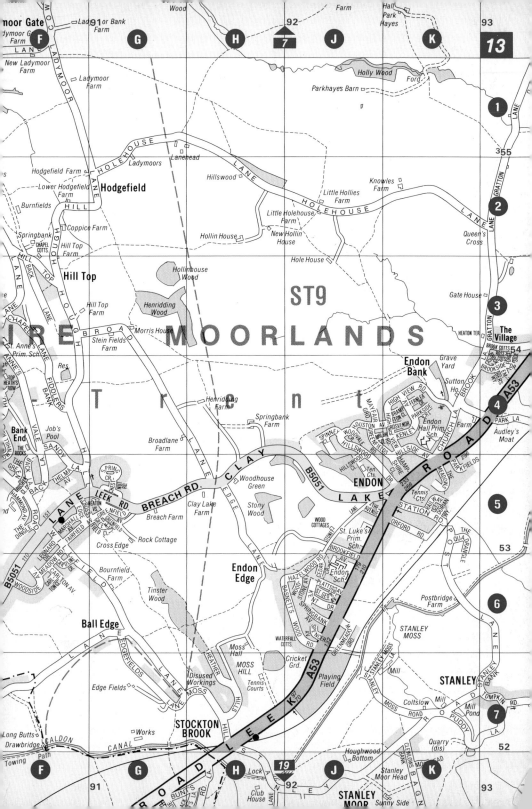

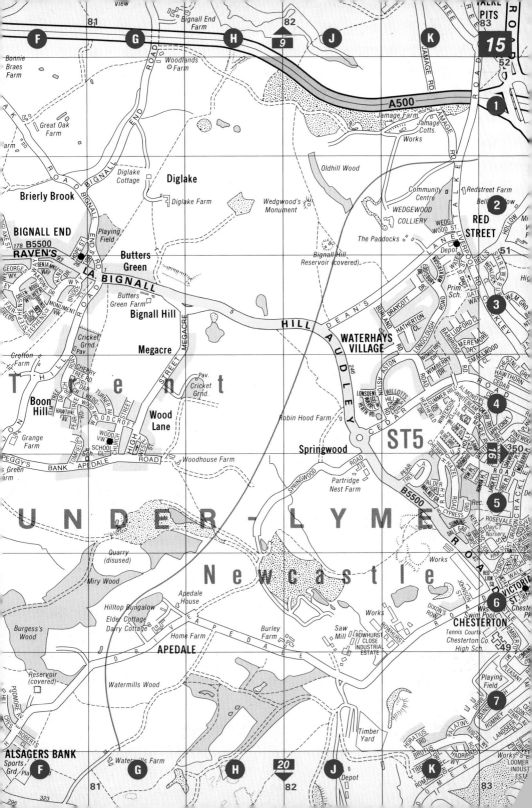

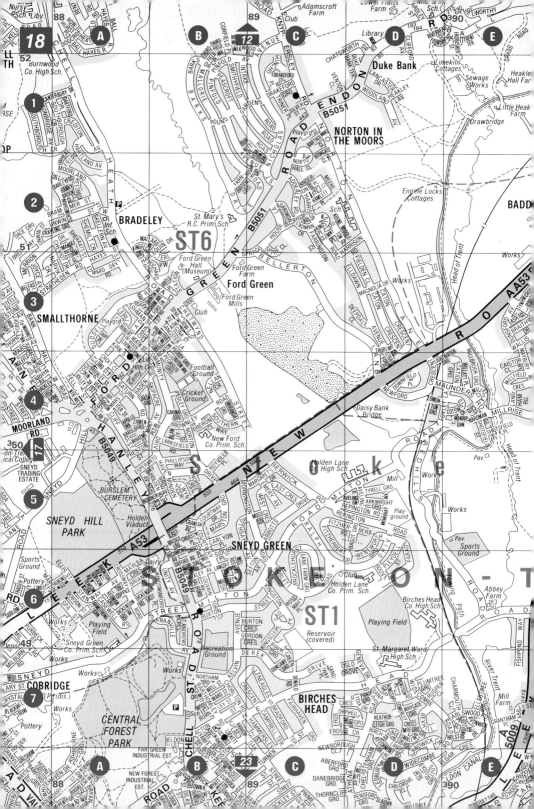

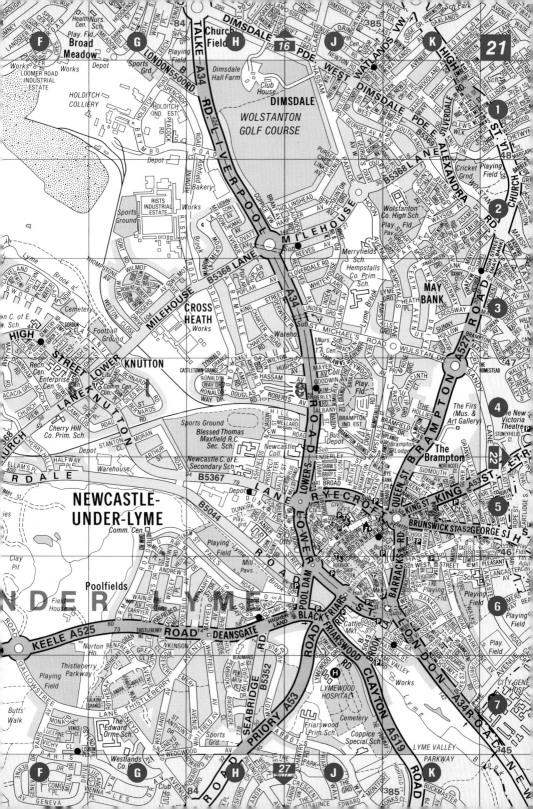

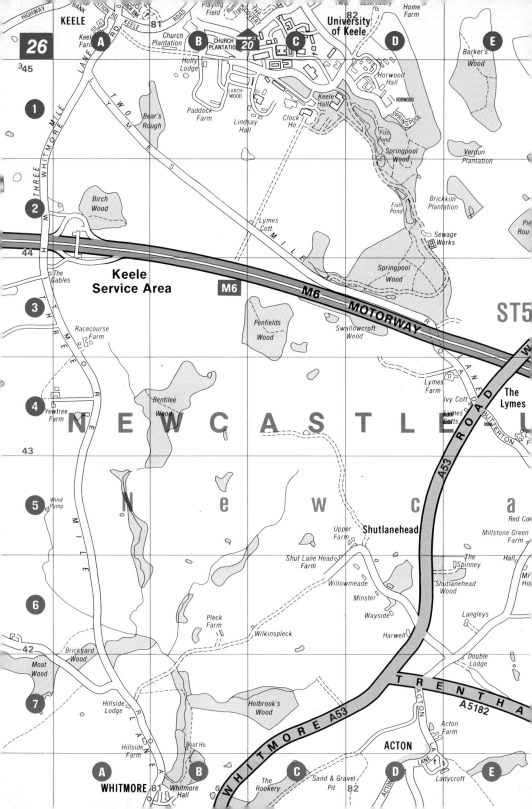

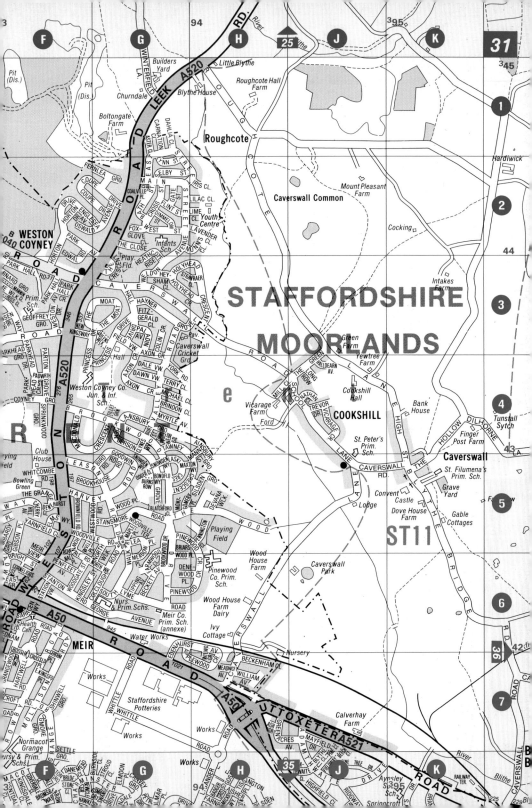

36
43
Caverswall
St. Filumena's Prim. Sch.
Grave Yard
Fair View
Gable Cottages
Tunstall Sytch
396
DILHORNE LANE
HOLLOW
Creswellford
Dilhorne House
The Croft
97
St. Thomas's Trees
A
B
C
D
E
1
2
3
4
5
6
7
Callowhill
Oaklea
ST10
BLYTHE BRIDGE ROAD
Light Railway
Field House
Kelson
Callowhill Wood
Cashheath
Foxfield
Exhibition Farm
Stoke-on-Trent
42
31
Moor Green Farm
CHAPEL
HORNE ROAD
A521 ROAD
Forsbrook Cemetery
Mount Pleasant
Heath House
Moor Green
CAVERSWALL ROAD
STAFFORDSHIRE
Newhouse Farm
QUABBS LANE
80
BLYTHE BRIDGE
River Blithe
RAILWAY TER.
Beeches Co. Jun. Sch. & Forsbrook Inf. Sch.
FORSBROOK
MOORLANDS
CHEADLE
DRAYCOTT OLD ROAD
Myrtle Grove
New Park
225
229
Blythe Bridge Co. High Sch.
Lib.
UTTOXETER ROAD
LANE
The Farm
188
192
Blythe Bridge
Mill Pond
Mill
Blythe Marsh
Recreation Ground
Hall
Cairneycroft
41
ST11
A521
Roman Road
457
Coach Depot
River Blithe
STALLINGTON
A50
Stonehouses
Marsh House
Marsh House Farm
Hawthorne Farm
Draycott Manor Co. Prim. Sch.
35
UTTOXETER ROAD
Roman Road
Woodlands
Higher Gorsty Birch
Gorstybirch
340
Lower Gorsty Birch
STAFFORD
Draycott Lodge
Little Leacroft Farm
River Blithe
Old Mill Race
Pumping Station
Cresswell
Station Farm
Sports Grd.
Pav.
Farm
CRESSWELL OLD
Stallington Sprink
396
97

INDEX TO STREETS

HOW TO USE THIS INDEX

1. Each name is followed by its Postcode District and then by its map reference, e.g. Aarons Dri. ST7—3F 15 is in the ST7 Postcode District and appears in map square 3F on Page 15. It is not recommended that this index be used as a means of addressing mail.

2. A strict alphabetical order is followed in which Avenue, Road, Street etc., (even though abbreviated) are read as part of the name preceding them e.g. Abbot's Way. appears after Abbots Rd. but before Abbotts Dri.

3. Street and subsidiary names not shown on the Maps, appear in *Italics* with the thoroughfare to which it is connected shown in brackets.

GENERAL ABBREVIATIONS

All : Alley	Cir : Circus	Gt : Great	M : Mews	Sta : Station
App : Approach	Clo : Close	Grn : Green	Mt : Mount	ST : Stoke
Arc : Arcade	Comn : Common	Gro : Grove	N : North	St : Street
Av : Avenue	Cotts : Cottages	Ho : House	Pal : Palace	Ter : Terrace
Bk : Back	Ct : Court	Ind : Industrial	Pde : Parade	Up : Upper
Boulevd : Boulevard	Cres : Crescent	Junct : Junction	Pk : Park	Vs : Villas
Bri : Bridge	Dri : Drive	La : Lane	Pas : Passage	Wlk : Walk
B'way : Broadway	E : East	Lit : Little	Pl : Place	W : West
Bldgs : Buildings	Embkmt : Embankment	L : Liverpool	Prom : Promenade	Yd : Yard
Bus : Business	Est : Estate	Lwr : Lower	Rd : Road	
Cen : Centre	Gdns : Gardens	Mans : Mansions	S : South	
Chyd : Churchyard	Ga : Gate	Mkt : Market	Sq : Square	

INDEX TO STREETS

Ashmore's La. ST7—1D 8
Ashmore Wlk. ST1—2G 23
(off Bucknall Old Rd.)
Ashridge Av. ST5—5J 27
Ashridge Gro. ST3—2C 30
Ashton Ct. ST5—5K 27
Ashton Ct. ST9—3F 25
Ashton St. ST3—4A 30
Ashurst Gro. ST3—1G 35
Ash Way. ST2—3E 24
Ashwell Rd. ST4—6A 22
Ashwood. ST3—2A 30
Ashwood Gro. ST11—5B 36
Ashwood Ter. ST3—2B 30
Ashworth St. ST4—1G 29
Aspen Gro. ST7—1G 11
Asquith Clo. ST8—3B 6
Astbury Clo. ST7—1E 10
Aster Clo. ST3—1G 31
Aston Rd. ST5—4K 15
Astro Gro. ST3—3K 29
Athelstan St. ST6—2F 17
Athena Rd. ST1—1J 23
Atherstone Rd. ST4—1D 32
Athlone St. ST6—3B 18
Atholl Rd. ST3—6C 30
Atlam Clo. ST2—3K 23
Atlantic Gro. ST4—7F 29
Atlas St. ST4—2H 29
Attwood Rise. ST7—2C 10
Attwood St. ST7—2C 10
Aubrey St. ST6—5D 10
Auckland St. ST6—5J 17
Auden Pl. ST3—3C 30
Audley Pl. ST5—2J 27
Audley Rd. ST5—3J 15
Audley Rd. ST7—2E 8
(Alsager)
Audley Rd. ST7—6G 9
(Talke Pits)
Audley St. ST5—3F 21
Audley St. ST6—2F 17
Austin Ho. ST2—2K 23
Austin St. ST1—4G 23
Austwick Gro. ST4—2B 28
Aveling Grn. ST1—5D 18
Aveling Rd. ST1—5D 18
Avenue Rd. ST4—5E 22
Avenue, The. ST5 & ST4—7A 22
(Newcastle, Hartshill)
Avenue, The. ST5—4A 22
(Newcastle, May Bank)
Avenue, The. ST7—7C 2
(Alsager)
Avenue, The. ST7—3B 10
(Kidsgrove)
Avenue, The. ST9—5J 13
Avenue, The. ST11—4B 36
Avion Clo. ST3—1H 35
Avoca St. ST1—1G 23
Avon Clo. ST5—3J 27
Avon Clo. ST7—2D 10
Avon Ct. ST7—6C 2
Avondale St. ST6—5F 17
Avonside Av. ST6—1H 17
Avonwick Gro. ST1—7E 18
Axbridge Wlk. ST6—4A 18
(off Kinver St.)
Axon Cres. ST4—4G 31
Aylesbury Rd. ST2—4B 24
Aynsley Av. ST5—4J 27
Aynsley Rd. ST4—5E 22
Aynsley's Dri. ST11—1K 35
Ayshford St. ST3—4A 30

Back Bunt's La. ST9—1H 19
Back Ford Grn. Rd. ST6—3B 18
Bk. Garden St. ST5—6K 21
Bk. Heathcote St. ST7—2C 10
Back La. ST5—5F & 3F 13
(in two parts)
Baddeley Grn. La. ST2—4F 19
Baddeley Hall Rd. ST2—3G 19
Baddeley Rd. ST2—4F 19
Baddeley St. ST6—4H 17
Baden Rd. ST6—4A 18
Baden St. ST5—4J 21
Badger Gro. ST3—1H 35
Baggott Pl. ST5—6G 21

Bagnall Rd. ST2—4F 19
(in two parts)
Bagnall Rd. ST9—1K 19
Bagnall St. ST1—3F 23
Bagot Gro. ST1—5D 18
Bailey Ct. ST7—7F 3
Bailey Rd. ST3—3H 29
Bailey St. ST4—5C 22
Bailey St. ST5—5H 21
Bainbridge Rd. ST4—1D 32
Bains Gro. ST5—5B 16
Baker Cres. ST2—2F 19
Baker Cres. N. ST2—2F 19
Baker Cres. S. ST2—2F 19
Baker St. ST4—1H 29
Bakewell Clo. ST5—5C 20
Bakewell St. ST4—2C 28
Balfour Gro. ST8—3C 6
Balfour St. ST1—3G 23
Ball Grn. La. ST6—6C 12
Ball Hayes Rd. ST6—7A 12
Ballinson Rd. ST3—6H 29
Balliol St. ST4—7D 22
Ball La. ST6—7E 12
Balloon St. ST4—5A 22
Balmoral Clo. ST4—5D 28
Baltic Clo. ST4—1E 32
Bamber Pl. ST5—7B 16
Bamber St. ST4—6E 22
Bambury St. ST3—1A 30
Bamford Gro. ST1—1E 22
Banbury Gro. ST8—4A 6
Banbury St. ST7—3K 9
Bancroft La. ST11—5A 36
Bank Ct. ST7—2C 10
(off Attwood St.)
Bankfield Rd. ST3—7E 30
Bank Hall Rd. ST6—3K 17
Bank Ho. Dri. ST5—4B 22
Bankhouse Rd. ST4—7C 28
Bankhouse Rd. ST11—3C 36
Bankside. ST5—6K 21
Bankside Ct. ST7—6E 2
Bank St. ST6—1F 17
Bank St. ST7—7E 4
Bank, The. ST7—4D 4
Bank Top Av. ST6—2J 17
Banky Brook Clo. ST6—2A 18
Barber Dri. ST7—4A 4
Barber Pl. ST6—6H 11
Barber Rd. ST6—6H 11
Barber Sq. ST5—2A 22
Barber St. ST6—4H 17
Barbridge Rd. ST5—3K 15
Barbrook Av. ST3—3D 30
Barclay St. ST3—2B 30
Barden St. ST5—4J 21
Bardsey Wlk. ST3—4K 29
Barford Rd. ST5—3G 27
Barford St. ST3—4A 30
Bargrave St. ST2—5C 24
Barker Ho. ST3—7J 29
Barker St. ST3—4C 30
Barker St. ST5—7B 16
Barks Dri. ST6—1B 18
Barlaston Old Rd. ST4 & ST12
—2E 32
Barlaston Rd. ST3—1J 33
Barley Croft. ST7—2E 8
Barleycroft Ter. ST7—4B 4
Barleyfields. ST6—2A 18
Barleyford Dri. ST3—1C 30
Barlow St. ST3—4B 30
Barlstone Av. ST11—5A 36
Barmouth Gro. ST8—2A 12
Barnbridge Clo. ST7—4A 4
Barncroft Rd. ST6—6K 11
Barnes Way. ST3—6B 30
Barnett Gro. ST6—7H 11
Barnfield. ST4—1C 28
Barnfield Rd. ST6—6J 17
Barnlea Gro. ST3—3F 35
Barnsdale Clo. ST4—3E 32
Barnwell Gro. ST4—6D 28
Baron St. ST4—2K 29
Barracks Rd. ST5—6K 21
Barracks Sq. ST5—6K 21
Barrage Rd. ST8—5F 7
Barratt Gdns. ST2—5F 19
Barratt Rd. ST7—1F 9
Barrett Cres. ST6—7J 17

Barrett Dri. ST6—7J 17
Barrie Gdns. ST7—4J 9
Barrington Ct. ST5—3A 22
Barry Av. ST2—3K 23
Bartholomew Rd. ST3—7E 30
Barthomley Rd. ST1—7B 18
Barthomley Rd. ST7—3A 14
Bartlem St. ST3—2C 30
Barton Cres. ST6—4G 17
Barwood Av. ST7—6G 3
Basford Pk. Rd. ST5—2A 22
Basildon Gro. ST3—5B 30
Baskerville Rd. ST1—1G 23
Baskeyfield Pl. ST6—7K 11
Basnett's Wood Rd. ST9—6J 13
Bassilow Rd. ST4—7J 23
Bateman Av. ST8—6K 5
Bath Rd. ST5—4A 20
Baths Pas. ST3—3A 30
(off The Strand)
Baths Rd. ST3—3A 30
Bath St. ST3—2G 31
Bath St. ST4—7D 22
Bath Ter. ST4—7D 22
Bathurst St. ST3—3B 30
Batten Clo. ST3—1H 35
Battison Cres. ST3—5A 30
Baulk La. ST11—7K 35
Bayham Wlk. ST2—2K 23
Baytree Clo. ST1—7D 18
Beaconsfield. ST5—6E 16
Beaconsfield Dri. ST3—6H 29
Beadnell Gro. ST8—6B 30
Beard Gro. ST2—6F 19
Beasley Av. ST5—7B 16
Beasley Pl. ST5—6B 16
Beatrice Wlk. ST8—2K 11
Beattie Av. ST5—3J 21
Beauford Av. ST9—3F 25
Beaufort Rd. ST3—5B 30
Beaulieu Clo. ST9—3G 25
Beaumaris Clo. ST4—6A 22
Beaumaris Ct. ST5—7H 21
Beaumont Clo. ST8—1B 6
Beaumont Rd. ST6—2G 17
Beaver Clo. ST4—3B 28
Beckenham Clo. ST3—7H 31
Beckett Av. ST3—6G 31
Beckfields Clo. ST8—2F 7
Beckford St. ST1—1G 23
Beckton Av. ST6—2G 17
Bedale Rd. ST6—6H 29
Bedcroft. ST12—6J 33
Bedford Cres. ST5—3K 27
Bedford Gro. ST7—6B 2
Bedford Rd. ST1—4E 22
Bedford St. ST7—1C 10
Bedford St. ST4—4D 22
Beech Av. ST7—3E 2
Beechcliff La. ST4 & ST12
—6A 32
Beech Clo. ST8—2F 7
Beech Ct. ST11—7J 31
Beechcroft Est. ST12—6J 33
Beech Dale Rd. ST4—7A 32
Beech Dri. ST7—4A 10
Beeches Row. ST6—7F 11
Beeches, The. ST5—6E 16
Beechfield Rd. ST4—2E 32
Beechfields. ST12—6J 33
Beech Gro. ST4—2F 29
Beech Gro. ST5—2K 21
Beech La. ST4—6A 32
Beechmont Gro. ST11—7D 18
Beech Rd. ST3—6J 29
Beech St. ST3—4B 30
Beechwood Clo. ST5—6A 28
Beechwood Clo. ST11—5A 36
Beechwood Dri. ST7—7B 2
Beeston Dri. ST7—1C 8
Beeston St. ST3—2B 30
Beeston View. ST7—5C 10
Belfast St. ST6—3K 17
Belfield Av. ST5—2K 21
Belford Pl. ST4—5C 22
Belgrave Rd. ST3—5A 30
Belgrave Av. ST7—6D 2
Belgrave Cres. ST3—6B 30
Belgrave Rd. ST3—6B 30
Belgrave Rd. ST5—6K 21
Bell Av. ST3—5C 30

Bellefield View. ST5—5A 22
(off High St., May Bank)
Bellerton La. ST6—3C 18
Bell Ho. ST3—1J 33
Bell La. ST12—4F 33
Bellringer Clo. ST8—4A 6
Bell's Hollow. ST5—3A 16
Bellwood Clo. ST3—3F 35
Belmont Rd. ST1—3D 22
Belsay Clo. ST3—3B 30
Belvedere Rd. ST4—6D 28
Belvedere Ter. ST7—4F 3
Belvoir Av. ST4—3F 33
Bemersley Rd. ST8 & ST6
—2A 12
Benedict Pl. ST2—1K 23
Benfleet Pl. ST3—4K 29
Bengal Gro. ST4—7F 29
Bengry Rd. ST3—5D 30
Benjamins Way. ST7—3F 15
Bennet Precinct. ST3—4A 30
Bennett Pl. ST5—6D 16
Bennett St. ST6—6G 17
Bennion St. ST3—4B 30
Benson St. ST6—7H 11
Bentley Av. ST5—2J 21
Bentley Rd. ST6—7A 12
Berdmore St. ST4—2K 29
Beresford Cres. ST5—1H 27
Beresford St. ST4—5E 22
Bergamot Dri. ST3—2F 35
Berkeley Av. ST7—6D 2
Berkeley Ct. ST5—5K 21
Berkeley St. ST1—3G 23
Berkshire Gro. ST5—2K 27
Bernard Gro. ST3—4E 34
Bernard St. ST1—3G 23
Berne Av. ST5—1F 27
Berryfield Gro. ST3—3E 30
Berry Hill Greenway. ST2
—4A 24
Berryhill-Normacot Greenway.
ST3—1C 30
Berry Hill Rd. ST4—5G 23
Berry La. ST3—4A 30
Berry St. ST4—7E 22
Berwick Rd. ST1—5C 18
Berwick Wlk. ST5—7G 21
Best St. ST4—2J 29
Beswick Rd. ST6—7H 11
Betchton La. ST7—3C 2
Betchton Rd. CW11—1A 2
Bethesda Rd. ST1—4G 23
Bethesda St. ST1—3F 23
Betley Pl. ST5—1K 27
Bettany Rd. ST6—6J 17
Bevan Av. ST7—6K 9
Bevendean Clo. ST4—3F 33
Beveridge Clo. ST3—5G 31
(off Brookwood Dri.)
Beverley Cres. ST11—3B 36
Beverley Rd. ST2—4A 24
Beville St. ST4—1H 29
Bevin La. ST2—3K 23
Bewcastle Gro. ST3—1F 35
Bew St. ST6—7C 12
Bexhill Gro. ST1—7D 18
Bexley St. ST1—1E 22
Bibbey St. ST7—4E 2
Biddulph Rd. ST6—6J 11
Biddulph Rd. ST7—5G 5
Bignall End Rd. ST7—2G 15
Bignall Hill. ST7—3G 15
Bigsbury Wlk. ST6—6J 17
(off Swainsley Clo.)
Billinge St. ST6—5G 17
Bilton St. ST4—1D 28
Birchall Av. ST6—7E 10
Bircham Wlk. ST5—5J 27
Birch Av. ST7—2E 8
Birch Av. ST8—5J 5
Birchdown Av. ST6—2K 17
Birchenwood Rd. ST6—3G 11
Birches Head Rd. ST1 & ST2
—1G 23 to 6E 18
Birchfield Av. ST7—4F 3
Birchfield Rd. ST2—1B 24
Birchgate. ST2—2B 24
Birchgate Gro. ST2—2B 24
Birch Grn. Gro. ST1—6C 18
Birch Gro. ST3—4F 35

Birch Gro. ST11—4B 36
Birch Ho. Rd. ST5—5K 15
Birchlands Rd. ST1—7D 18
Birchover Way. ST6—4J 11
Birch Rd. ST7—4F 15
Birch St. ST1—1H 23
Birch Ter. ST1—3F 23
Birch Tree La. ST7—4D 4
Birch Wlk. ST3—6K 29
Bird Cage Wlk. ST1—3F 23
Bird Rd. ST3—5G 31
Birkdale Dri. ST7—1E 10
Birkholme Dri. ST3—3F 35
Birks St. ST4—2E 28
Birrell St. ST4—2J 29
Biscay Gro. ST4—7F 29
Bishop Rd. ST6—7J 11
Bishop's Clo. ST7—4K 9
Bishop St. ST4—2K 29
Bitterne Pl. ST2—6C 24
Blackbank Rd. ST5—3C 20
Blackfriars Rd. ST5—6J 21
Black Horse La. ST1—2F 23
Blacklake Dri. ST3—4F 35
Blackthorn Pl. ST5—5A 16
Blackwell's Row. ST6—7K 17
Blackwood Pl. ST3—3D 30
Bladon Av. ST5—4J 27
Bladon Clo. ST6—4J 11
Bladon Cres. ST7—6C 2
Blakelow Rd. ST2—1A 24
Blakeney Av. ST5—4J 27
Blake St. ST6—5H 17
Blanchard Clo. ST3—1H 35
Blantyre St. ST3—5B 30
Blantyre Wlk. ST3—5B 30
Blatchford Clo. ST3—5G 31
Bleak Pl. ST6—6J 17
Bleak St. ST5—3A 22
Blencarn Gro. ST9—1G 19
Blenheim Ct. ST7—7D 2
Blenheim St. ST4—2G 29
Bleriot Clo. ST3—1H 35
Blithe View. ST11—5A 36
Blithfield Clo. ST9—4F 25
Bluestone Av. ST6—3K 17
Blunt St. ST5—2K 21
Blurton Rd. ST4 & ST3—3H 29
  (Stoke-on-Trent)
Blurton St. ST12 & ST3—6K 33
  (Barlaston)
Blythe Av. ST3—3F 35
Blythe Bri. Rd. ST11—5K 31
Blythe Clo. ST11—1J 35
Blythe Mt. Pk. ST11—4B 36
Blythe Rd. ST11—4B 36
Boardmans Bank. ST6—3E 12
Boat Horse Rd. ST6—6C 10
Boathorse Rd. ST7—4B 10
Bodmin Wlk. ST6—4B 18
  (off Community Dri.)
Bogs La. ST11—5A 36
Bold St. ST1—1G 23
Bolina Gro. ST3—1A 30
Bollin Clo. ST7—1A 8
Bollin Gro. ST8—2C 6
Bolney Gro. ST1—1J 23
Bolsover Clo. ST6—4J 11
Bolton Pl. ST3—7E 30
Boma Rd. ST4—7C 28
Bondfield Way. ST3—5G 31
Bond St. ST6—1F 17
Bonnard Clo. ST3—2H 35
Bonner Clo. ST4—2B 28
Boon Av. ST4—1D 28
Boon Hill Rd. ST7—4F 15
Boothen Ct. ST4—2D 28
Boothen Grn. ST4—2E 28
Boothen Old Rd. ST4—2E 28
Boothen Rd. ST4—1E 28
  (in two parts)
Boothenwood Ter. ST4—2D 28
Boothroyd St. ST1—3F 23
Booth St. ST4—1E 28
Booth St. ST5—7B 16
Booth St. ST7—3D 14
Borough Rd. ST5—5K 21
Borrowdale Rd. ST6—2C 18
Boscombe Gro. ST4—3F 33
Bosinney Clo. ST4—2A 30
Bosley Gro. ST6—5E 10

Boswell St. ST4—4C 22
Botany Bay Rd. ST1—1H 23
Botteslow St. ST1—3G 23
Boughey Rd. ST4—6F 23
Boughey Rd. ST7—3F 15
Boughey St. ST4—1D 28
Boulevard, The. ST6—2G 17
Boulton St. ST1—1G 23
Boulton St. ST5—7E 16
Boundary Ct. ST1—1F 23
  (off Union St.)
Boundary St. ST1—1E 22
Boundary St. ST5—5A 22
Bourne Rd. ST7—2B 10
Bournes Bank. ST6—5H 17
Bourne St. ST4—3H 29
Bourne St. ST7—4F 5
Bouverie Pde. ST1—6D 18
Bowden St. ST6—4K 17
Bower St. ST1—4F 23
Bowfell Gro. ST3—1A 30
Bowland Av. ST5—3F 21
Bowman Gro. ST6—5K 11
Bowman Ho. ST3—7E 30
Bowmead Clo. ST4—2F 22
Bowness St. ST1—1E 22
Bowstead St. ST4—7E 22
Bow St. ST1—1F 23
Bowyer Av. ST6—7C 12
Box La. ST3—5E 30
Boxwood Pl. ST5—5K 15
Boyles Hall Rd. ST7—3E 14
Brabazon Clo. ST3—1H 35
Brackenberry. ST5—3J 21
Bracken Clo. ST3—3E 34
Bracken Clo. ST7—3F 3
Bracken Clo. ST12—7D 32
Brackenfield Av. ST2—5B 24
Brackens, The. ST5—5K 27
Bracken St. ST4—3H 29
Brackley Av. ST6—4K 17
Bradbury Clo. ST6—2C 18
Bradford Ter. ST1—7C 18
Bradwell Grange. ST5—6D 16
Bradwell La. ST5—5B 16
Bradwell Lodge. ST5—7E 16
Bradwell St. ST6—5F 17
Braemar Clo. ST2—3C 24
Braemore Rd. ST2—7F 19
Braithwell Dri. ST2—3E 18
Brakespeare St. ST6—5E 10
Brake, The. ST7—4D 4
Brake Village. ST7—4D 4
Bramber St. ST4—6E 22
Brambles, The. ST5—5K 27
Bramfield Dri. ST6—4K 21
Bramley Pl. ST4—5B 28
Brammall Dri. ST11—1K 35
Brammer St. ST6—2A 18
Brampton Clo. ST9—4K 13
Brampton Ct. ST5—4K 21
Brampton Gdns. ST5—3K 21
Brampton Ind. Est. ST5—4J 21
Brampton Rd. ST5—4K 21
Brampton Sidings. ST5—4J 21
Brampton Wlk. ST3—6B 30
Brandon Gro. ST4—7C 28
Branson Av. ST4—3D 30
Bransty Gro. ST4—3F 33
Brant Av. ST5—2H 21
Brassington Way. ST2—5B 24
Brattswood Dri. ST7—6G 3
Breach Rd. ST6—5G 13
Bream Way. ST6—3K 17
Brecon Way. ST4—2B 24
Breedon Clo. ST5—3G 21
Breeze Av. ST6—1G 17
Brendale Clo. ST4—6D 28
Brentnor Clo. ST3—4E 30
Brentwood Dri. ST9—2G 25
Brentwood Gro. ST9—2G 19
Brereton Pl. ST6—4G 17
Bretherton Pl. ST6—6J 11
Brewery St. ST1—2F 23
Brewester Rd. ST2—3J 23
Brianson Av. ST6—6A 18
Briarbank Clo. ST4—6C 28
Briars, The. ST5—4J 21
Briarswood. ST7—3D 10
Briarswood Pl. ST3—5G 31
Brickfield Pl. ST3—1B 30

Brick Ho. St. ST6—5H 17
Brickkiln La. ST4—5B 22
Brick Kiln La. ST5—6A 16
Bridestone Clo. ST3—1F 35
Bridge Clo. ST7—3F 15
Bridge Ct. ST4—4B 28
Bridge Croft. ST6—6K 11
Bridge Rd. ST4—4B 28
Bridge St. ST5—5J 21
  (Newcastle)
Bridge St. ST5—5D 20
  (Silverdale)
Bridge St. ST8—2K 11
Bridgett Clo. ST4—2B 28
Bridgewater St. ST6—5F 17
Bridgewood St. ST3—4B 30
Bridgnorth Gro. ST5—3A 16
Bridgwood St. ST11—4B 36
Bridle Path. ST7—2F 25
Bridle Path. ST3—6B 30
  (off Peel St.)
Bridle Path, The. ST5—4G 27
Brierley St. ST6—4A 18
Brieryhurst Clo. ST2—1B 24
Brieryhurst Rd. ST7—1D 10
Brightgreen St. ST3—1C 30
Brighton St. ST4—7D 22
Brighton, The. ST5—4C 20
Bright St. ST3—6F 31
Brindiwell Gro. ST4—2F 22
Brindley Clo. ST4—4A 10
Brindley La. ST2—2G 19
Brindley Pl. ST6—6A 12
Brindley St. ST5—5J 21
Brindleys Way. ST7—3F 15
Brindon Clo. ST3—4G 31
Brinscall Grn. ST6—5J 11
  (off Charnock Pl.)
Brinsley Av. ST4—2D 32
Brisley Hill. ST4—1C 28
Bristol St. ST5—1A 22
Britannia Pk. Ind. Est. ST6
  —6K 17
Brittain Av. ST5—6A 16
Brittle Pl. ST6—3B 18
Britton St. ST4—5C 22
Brixham Clo. ST2—5J 23
Broadfield Rd. ST6—5D 10
Broadhurst St. ST6—4K 17
Broad La. ST6—3G 13
Broadlawns Dri. ST3—1A 36
Broadmine St. ST4—1J 29
Broadoak Way. ST3—6H 29
Broad St. ST1—4E 22
Broad St. ST5—5J 21
  (in two parts)
Broadway. ST3—5E 30
Broadway Ct. ST3—6E 30
Broadway Pl. ST3—5E 30
Brockbank Pl. ST6—7K 11
Brocklehurst Way. ST1—6C 18
Brockley Sq. ST1—2F 23
Brocksford St. ST4—2K 29
Brocton Wlk. ST3—6H 29
Brogan St. ST1—1J 29
Bromley Ct. ST1—1E 22
Bromley Hough. ST4—2C 28
Bromley St. ST1—1D 22
Brompton Dri. ST2—2F 19
Bromsberrow Way. ST3
  —1F 35
Bromsgrove Pl. ST3—4K 29
Bronant Wlk. ST6—6J 17
  (off Leonora St.)
Brook Clo. ST9—4K 13
Brook Clo. ST11—4B 36
Brook Cotts. ST9—4K 13
Brooke Pl. ST5—2K 27
Brookfield Av. ST9—5J 13
Brookfield Ct. ST1—1F 23
  (off Union St.)
Brookfield Dri. ST7—6C 2
Brookfield Rd. ST2—2G 19
Brookfield Rd. ST4—2B 28
Brook Gdns. ST8—2B 6
Brookgate. ST1—1D 22
Brookhouse Dri. ST12—6F 33
Brookhouse La. ST2—3C 24
Brookhouse Rd. ST3—5F 31
Brookhouse Rd. ST5—4B 16
Brookhouse Rd. ST7—1D 8

Brookland Rd. ST6—7H 11
Brooklands Av. ST3—6K 29
Brooklands Cotts. ST6—4G 11
Brook La. ST5—6J 21
Brook La. ST9—4K 13
Brookmead Gro. ST3—1A 30
Brook Pl. ST4—5C 22
Brook Rd. ST4—1D 32
Brookside. ST6—5F 17
Brookside Clo. ST5—7H 21
Brookside Dri. ST3—5H 29
Brookside Dri. ST9—4K 13
Brook St. ST4—7E 22
Brook St. ST5—4D 20
Brook St. ST8—6J 5
Brookview Dri. ST3—4E 30
Brook Vs. ST7—1E 8
Brookwood Clo. ST5—4J 27
Brookwood Dri. ST3—4F 31
Broome Hill. ST5—6K 27
Broomfield Pl. N. ST1—3D 22
Broomfield P. S. ST1—3D 22
Broomfield Rd. ST6—7B 12
Broomfields. ST7—4J 9
Broomhill St. ST6—1E 16
Broom St. ST1—1G 23
Brough La. ST4—1E 32
Broughton Cres. ST12—6H 33
Broughton Rd. ST2—3K 23
Broughton Rd. ST5—4A 22
Brown Av. ST7—7G 3
Brownfield Rd. ST3—5F 31
Brownhill Rd. ST6—5F 13
Brownhills Rd. ST6—4F 17
Browning Gro. ST7—4J 9
Browning Rd. ST3—5J 29
Brown Lees Rd. ST8—6K 5
  (Brown Lees)
Brown Lees Rd. ST8—7H 5
  (Harriseahead)
Brownley Rd. ST6—4B 18
Brownsea Pl. ST3—3H 29
Brown St. ST6—5J 17
Brundall Oval. ST2—4C 24
Brunel Wlk. ST3—3B 30
  (off Anchor Rd.)
Brunswick Pl. ST1—3F 23
Brunswick St. ST1—2F 23
Brunswick St. ST5—5K 21
Brunt St. ST6—6F 17
Brutus Rd. ST5—1E 20
Bryan St. ST1—2F 23
Bryant Rd. ST2—1A 24
Brymbo Rd. ST5—1G 21
Buccleuch Rd. ST3—5C 30
Buckingham Cres. ST4—6D 28
Buckland Gro. ST4—3F 33
Buckley Rd. ST6—6A 12
Buckley's Row. ST5—6J 21
Buckmaster Av. ST5—1K 25
Bucknall New Rd. ST1—2G 23
Bucknall Old Rd. ST1—2G 23
Bucknall Rd. ST1—3J 23
Bude Clo. ST7—1B 8
Buller St. ST1—4G 23
Bull La. ST8—2J 11
Bullocks Ho. Rd. ST7—1G 11
Bulstrode St. ST6—5G 17
Bunny Hill. ST5—2K 27
Bunt's La. ST9—1G 19
Buren St. ST6—2F 17
Burford Way. ST2—5K 23
Burgess St. ST6—6G 17
Burland Rd. ST5—3K 15
Burleigh Gro. ST5—3A 22
Burlidge Rd. ST6—6J 11
Burlington Av. ST5—3A 22
Burmarsh Wlk. ST6—6H 17
Burnaby Rd. ST6—6E 10
Burnett Pl. ST6—1B 18
Burnham St. ST4—2K 29
Burnhayes Rd. ST6—3H 17
Burnley St. ST1—7B 18
Burns Clo. ST7—4C 10
Burnside Clo. ST3—1F 35
Burns Row. ST3—1C 30
Burnwood Pl. ST6—7K 11
Burrington Dri. ST4—3E 32
Burslem Greenway. ST6
  —4H 17
Burslem Walkway. ST6—5J 17

Bursley Rd. ST6—6J 17
Bursley Way. ST5—5C 16
Burton Cres. ST1—6B 18
Burton Pl. ST1—2F 23
Burt St. ST3—4G 31
Bute St. ST4—3K 29
Butler St. ST4—1E 28
Butterfield Pl. ST6—2G 17
Buttermere Clo. ST6—5G 17
Butterton La. ST5—4E 26
Butts Grn. ST2—7G 19
Butts, The. ST7—7D 2
Buxton Av. ST5—4B 20
Buxton St. ST1—6B 18
Byatt's Gro. ST3—5K 29
Bycars La. ST6—4H 17
Bycars Rd. ST6—4H 17
Bylands Pl. ST5—2H 27
Byron Ct. ST7—4C 10
Byron St. ST4—5A 22
Bywater Gro. ST3—1C 30

Cadeby Gro. ST2—3F 19
Cadman Cres. ST6—2C 18
Cairn Clo. ST2—3C 24
Caistor Clo. ST2—4E 18
Caldbeck Pl. ST1—2G 23
Caldew Gro. ST4—3F 33
Caldy Rd. ST7—7C 2
Caledonia Rd. ST4—5E 22
California St. ST3—4K 29
Callender Pl. ST6—5J 17
Calvary Cres. ST2—6C 24
Calverley St. ST3—5C 30
Calver St. ST6—2F 17
Calvert Gro. ST5—6D 16
Camberwell Gro. ST4—2F 22
Camborne Cres. ST5—2G 27
Cambridge Ct. ST5—3A 28
Cambridge Dri. ST5—2A 28
Cambridge St. ST1—3E 22
Camden St. ST4—3H 29
Camelot Clo. ST4—3F 33
Camillus Rd. ST4—4F 21
Camoys Rd. ST6—6J 17
Campbell Pl. ST4—7E 22
Campbell Rd. ST4—3E 28
Campbell Ter. ST1—7C 18
Campion Av. ST5—3A 22
Camp Rd. ST6—4A 18
Canal La. ST6—3F 17
Canal Side. ST12—7G 33
Canal St. ST6—5F 17
Canberra Cres. ST3—1H 35
Canning St. ST4—2J 29
Cannon Pl. ST1—4E 22
Cannon St. ST1—3F 23
Canterbury Dri. ST6—1K 17
Canvey Gro. ST3—1G 35
Capesthorne Clo. ST7—1C 6
Capesthorne Clo. ST9—3G 25
Cape St. ST1—1F 23
Capewell St. ST3—3B 30
Capper Clo. ST7—2C 10
Cappers La. CW11—1A 2
Capper St. ST6—2G 17
Capricorn Way. ST6—6H 11
Caraway Pl. ST3—2F 35
Carberry Way. ST3—3E 30
Cardiff Gro. ST1—4F 23
Cardigan Gro. ST4—2F 33
Cardington Clo. ST5—3H 27
Card St. ST6—6J 17
Cardway. ST5—6D 16
Cardwell St. ST1—1H 23
Carina Gdns. ST6—4B 18
Carisbrooke Way. ST4—3F 33
Carling Gro. ST4—2K 29
Carlisle St. ST3—6A 30
Carlton Av. ST5—4J 27
Carlton Av. ST6—6F 13
(Brown Edge)
Carlton Av. ST6—1J 17
(Stoke-on-Trent)
Carlton Clo. ST6—6F 13
Carlton Rd. ST4—6F 23
Carlyon Pl. ST1—5B 18
Carmount Rd. ST2—6F 19
Carnation Clo. ST3—1G 31
Carnforth Gro. ST6—4G 11

Caroline Clo. ST9—2G 25
Caroline Cres. ST6—6F 13
Caroline St. ST3—3B 30
Carols Pl. ST5—4D 16
Carpenter Rd. ST3—3K 29
Carrick Pl. ST4—4F 23
Carriage Dri. ST8—2C 6
Carrick Rd. ST4—6D 28
Carr La. ST7—4A 14
Carroll Dri. ST3—3C 30
Carron St. ST4—2A 30
Carr St. ST7—3H 11
Carryer Pl. ST5—6G 21
Carson Rd. ST6—2H 17
Cartlich St. ST6—7F 11
Cartlidge St. ST4—5A 22
Cartmel Pl. ST6—2K 17
Cartwright St. ST3—4B 30
Casewell Rd. ST6—6A 18
Caspian Gro. ST4—1E 32
Castel Clo. ST5—4F 27
Castledine Gro. ST3—3C 30
Castlefield St. ST4—4D 22
Castle Hill Rd. ST5—5H 21
Castle Ridge. ST5—6G 21
Castle Rd. ST7—4F 5
Castle St. ST5—6A 16
(Chesterton)
Castle St. ST5—5K 21
(Newcastle)
Castleton Rd. ST3—1D 34
Castletown Grange. ST5
—4H 21
Castle View. ST8—5A 6
Castle View Gro. ST6—4G 11
Castle View Rd. ST7—1D 10
Catalina Pl. ST3—2H 35
Caterham Pl. ST3—2G 35
Catharine Rd. ST6—6K 11
Catherine St. ST5—2A 22
Caton Cres. ST6—3D 18
Cauldon Av. ST5—6C 16
Cauldon Pl. ST1—5E 22
Cauldon Rd. ST4—5E 22
Caulton St. ST6—4H 17
Causeley Gdns. ST2—3A 24
Causeley Rd. ST2—3A 24
Cavendish Cres. ST7—6C 2
Cavendish Gro. ST5—4J 27
Cavendish St. ST1—3D 22
Caverswall La. ST3—6H 31
Caverswall Old Rd. ST11
—3A 36
Caverswall Rd. ST3—3G 31
Caverswall Rd. ST11—4A 36
(Blythe Bridge)
Caverswall Rd. ST11—5J 31
(Caverswall)
Cavour St. ST1—4C 22
Cayley Pl. ST3—2H 35
Cecil Av. ST1—1E 22
Cecil Rd. ST8—1A 6
Cedar Av. ST7—1C 8
(Alsager)
Cedar Av. ST7—3K 9
(Talke)
Cedar Av. ST11—5B 36
Cedar Ct. ST7—7E 2
Cedar Cres. ST7—4F 15
Cedar Cres. ST9—6J 13
Cedar Gro. ST3—4H 29
Cedar Gro. ST8—2E 6
Cedar Rd. ST5—4J 15
Cellarhead Rd. ST9—2J 25
Celtic Av. ST7—4H 11
Cemetery Av. ST3—5A 30
Cemetery Rd. ST4—4D 22
Cemetery Rd. ST5—3F 21
(Newcastle, Knutton)
Cemetery Rd. ST5—5E 20
(Newcastle, Silverdale)
Cemetery View. ST3—5A 30
Cemetery View. ST5—3F 21
Cemlyn Av. ST3—4H 29
Central Av. ST2—2A 30
Central Dri. ST3—4H 29
Central St. ST7—5D 4
Centre Ct. ST7—7E 2
Century St. ST1—1D to 2E 22
(in two parts)
Chadwell Way. ST2—5C 24
Chadwick St. ST3—4B 30

Chadwyn Dri. ST2—3F 19
Chaffinch Dri. ST8—3C 6
Chain St. ST6—3A 18
Chalfont Grn. ST2—4B 24
Challinor St. ST6—2G 17
Chamberlain Av. ST4—1D 28
Chamberlain St. ST1—4F 23
Chamberlain Way. ST8—3C 6
Chance Hall La. ST7—3H 3
Chancery La. ST3—4B 30
Chancery La. ST7—1B 8
Chantry Rd. ST5—7J 22
Chapel Bank. ST7—5F 5
Chapel Clo. ST7—5D 4
Chapel Cotts. ST6—2F 13
Chapel Ct. ST5—4D 20
Chapel La. ST6—3F 13
(Brown Edge)
Chapel La. ST6—5H 17
(Stoke-on-Trent)
Chapel La. ST7—3D 14
(Audley)
Chapel La. ST7—7G 5
(Harriseahead)
Chapel La. ST7—4F 3
(Rode Heath)
Chapel La. ST8—3E 6
Chapel St. ST2—2A 24
Chapel St. ST5—3F 21
(Knutton)
Chapel St. ST5—3K 21
(May Bank)
Chapel St. ST5—4D 20
(Silverdale)
Chapel St. ST7—2E 14
(Bignall End)
Chapel St. ST7—5D 4
(Mow Cop)
Chapel St. ST7—2K 9
(Talke)
Chapel St. ST11—3B 36
Chaplin Rd. ST3—6B 30
Chapter Wlk. ST2—1K 23
Charles Sq. CW11—1A 2
Charles St. ST1—3F 23
Charles St. ST5—3A 22
Charles St. ST8—4A 6
Charlotte St. ST6—5E 10
Charlton St. ST4—6E 22
Charminster Rd. ST3—1F 35
Charmouth Rd. ST1—7E 18
Charnock Pl. ST6—5J 11
Charnwood. ST7—3D 10
Charnwood Rd. ST3—6E 30
Charsley Pl. ST3—6J 29
Charter Rd. ST5—3H 21
Chartley Clo. ST11—2K 35
Chartwell Clo. ST9—3F 25
Chase Wlk. ST3—1E 34
Chatfield Pl. ST3—5C 30
Chatham St. ST1—4E 22
Chatsworth Dri. ST6—7D 12
Chatsworth Dri. ST9—4F 25
Chatsworth Pl. ST3—6E 30
Chatsworth Pl. ST5—6B 16
Chatteris Clo. ST3—2G 35
Chatterley Clo. ST5—5D 16
Chatterley Dri. ST7—5C 10
Chatterley Rd. ST6—1D 16
Chatterley St. ST6—3H 17
Chatterton Pl. ST3—4C 30
Chaucer Courts. ST3—6A 30
Cheadle Rd. ST11—4B 36
Cheapside. ST1—2F 23
Cheapside. ST5—6J 21
Checkley Dri. ST8—2B 6
Checkley Gro. ST3—1C 30
Cheddar Dri. ST5—4A 20
Chell Grn. Av. ST6—6J 11
Chell Grn. Ct. ST6—6J 11
Chell Gro. ST5—6C 16
Chell Heath Rd. ST6
—6K 11 to 3B 18
Chells Hill. CW11—2D 2
Chell St. ST1—1G 23
Chelmorton Dri. ST3—6D 30
Chelmsford Dri. ST2—4B 24
Chelmsford Rd. ST3—1J 21
Chelson St. ST3—4B 30
Cheltenham Gro. ST1—1J 23
Cheltenham Gro. ST5—4A 20

Chelwood St. ST1—1E 22
Chemical La. ST6—3D 16
Chemical La. Ind. Est. ST6
—4E 16
Chepstow Pl. ST3—1B 30
Cheriton Grn. ST2—5C 24
Cherry Clo. ST5—4K 15
Cherry Clo. ST11—7K 35
Cherry Gro. ST3—4H 29
Cherryhill Av. ST3—5F 31
Cherry Hill La. ST5—4F 21
Cherry La. ST7—5C 2
Cherry Orchard. ST5—5K 21
Cherry Tree Av. ST7—6G 3
Cherry Tree Clo. ST4—1D 32
Cherry Tree La. ST8—2E 6
Cherry Tree Rd. ST5—4A 20
Cherry Tree Rd. ST7—4F 15
Cherrywood Gro. ST3—2E 34
Chertsey Pl. ST1—5B 18
Chervil Clo. ST3—2F 35
Chesham Gro. ST3—2F 35
Chessington Cres. ST4—1F 33
Chester Clo. ST7—5A 10
Chester Cres. ST5—2H 27
Chester Rd. ST7—3D 14
(Audley)
Chester Rd. ST7—5K 9
(Talke)
Chesterwood Rd. ST6—2K 17
Chestnut Av. ST4—5B 28
Chestnut Av. ST7—4F 3
Chestnut Cres. ST11—5B 36
Chestnut Dri. ST7—2E 8
Chestnut Gro. ST5—4A 16
Chestnut Rd. ST6—5G 13
Chetwynd Av. ST2—2F 19
Chetwynd Av. ST6—7C 12
Chetwynd Rd. ST5—7D 16
Chetwynd St. ST5—1A 22
Chetwynd St. ST6—3B 18
Cheviot Clo. ST5—3F 21
Cheviot Dri. ST6—2A 18
Chichester Wlk. ST1—1G 23
Childerplay Rd. ST8—1A 12
Chilgrove Clo. ST1—1J 23
Chiltern Pl. ST5—3F 21
Chilton St. ST4—3H 29
Chilworth Gro. ST3—6J 29
China St. ST4—2J 29
Chivelstone Gro. ST4—2F 33
Choleton Clo. ST4—2H 29
Chorley Av. ST6—6J 11
Chorlton Rd. ST1—7B 18
Christchurch St. ST4—1H 29
Christie Pl. ST3—2E 30
Christine St. ST2—3K 23
Chubb Way. ST4—3B 28
Chumleigh Gro. ST6—3J 17
Church Av. ST2—3F 19
Church Bank. ST5—7A 20
Church Bank. ST7—3D 14
Church Clo. ST3—3E 34
Church Clo. ST8—5B 6
Church Dri. ST12—6H 33
Churchfield Av. ST3—6B 30
Church Fields. ST5—7A 20
Churchill Av. ST4—1C 32
Churchill Clo. ST11—2K 35
Churchill Ho. ST1—4F 23
Churchill Way. ST4—1C 32
Church La. ST4—5C 28
Church La. ST5—5F 21
(Knutton)
Church La. ST5—2A 22
(Wolstanton)
Church La. ST7—7J 3
(Church Lawton)
Church La. ST7—4G 5
(Mow Cop)
Church La. ST7—3H 3
(Scholar Green)
Church La. ST8—2F 7
Church La. ST9—4K 13
Church Plantation. ST5—7B 20
Church Rd. ST3—6J 29
Church Rd. ST6—3E 12
Church Rd. ST7—7B 2
Church Rd. ST8—4B 6
Church Sq. ST6—5G 17
Church St. ST4—7E 22

Church St. ST5—6A 16
(Chesterton)
Church St. ST5—5J 21
(Newcastle)
Church St. ST5—4C 20
(Silverdale)
Church St. ST7—3D 14
(Audley)
Church St. ST7—4G 15
(Bignall End)
Church St. ST7—5E 4
(Mow Cop)
Church St. ST7—7E 4
(Rookery)
Church St. ST7—2K 9
(Talke)
Church Ter. ST6—7K 17
Church View. ST5—4F 21
Church Wlk. ST5—6A 16
Churnet Rd. ST11—4B 36
Churston Clo. ST5—5J 27
Churston Pl. ST1—5B 18
Cinder Hill. ST2—4H 19
Cinderhill Ind. Est. ST3—3E 30
Cinderhill La. ST3—4C 30
Cinder-Hill La. ST7—5A 4
City Bank. ST8—1A 6
City Rd. ST4—7F 23
Clandon Av. ST6—1G 17
Clanway St. ST6—7F 11
Clare Av. ST5—7D 16
Claremont Clo. ST5—6E 16
Clarence Rd. ST3—3A 30
Clarence St. ST4—1H 29
Clarence St. ST5—6A 22
(Newcastle)
Clarence St. ST5—1J 21
(Wolstanton)
Clarendon St. ST4—1F 29
Clare St. ST4—5A 22
Clare St. ST7—7G 5
(Harriseahead)
Clare St. ST7—5E 4
(Mow Cop)
Claridge Rd. ST4—5B 22
Clarke St. ST1—4E 22
Claud St. ST4—3G 29
Claydon Cres. ST5—5J 27
Clayfield Gro. ST3—1B 30
Clayfield Gro. W. ST3—1A 30
Clayhanger Clo. ST5—5C 16
Clayhanger St. ST6—5H 17
Clay Hills. ST6—2E 16
Clay Lake. ST9—5H 13
Clayton La. ST4 & ST5—3K 27
Clayton Rd. ST5
—7J 21 to 6K 27
Clayton St. ST3—4A 30
Claytonwood Rd. ST4—4B 28
Cleadon Pl. ST2—7F 19
Clematis Av. ST11—5A 36
Clement Pl. ST6—2C 18
Clement Rd. ST6—7J 11
Clermont Av. ST4—5D 28
Cleveland Rd. ST1—4F 23
Cleveland St. ST5—3F 21
Cleveland St. ST6—5H 17
Clewlow Pl. ST3—2B 30
Clewlows Bank. ST9—7K 13
Clews St. ST6—6G 17
Clews Wlk. ST5—1K 21
Cley Gro. ST5—5J 27
Cliffe Pl. ST6—2J 17
Clifford Av. ST6—7D 12
Clifford St. ST1—4G 23
Cliff St. ST6—4A 18
Cliff Vale Pl. ST4—5C 22
Clifton Clo. ST4—2H 29
Clifton St. ST4—2H 29
Clifton St. ST5—2A 22
Clinton Sq. ST1—3F 23
Clive Av. ST2—2F 19
Cliveden Pl. ST3—5B 30
Cliveden Rd. ST2—1A 24
Clive Rd. ST5—7F 17
Clive St. ST6—1G 17
Cloister Wlk. ST2—1K 23
Close La. ST7—7A 2
(Alsager)
Close La. ST7—4F 5
(Mow Cop)

Close, The. ST3—2G 31
Close, The. ST7—1A 8
Clough Hall Dri. ST7—5A 10
Clough Hall Rd. ST7—4B 10
Clough La. ST9—3F 25
Clough St. ST1—3D 22
Clovelly Wlk. ST6—6G 17
Cloverdale Pl. ST3—4E 30
Cloverdale Rd. ST5—3J 21
Clover Rd. ST5—7F 17
Clowes Av. ST7—1F 9
Clowes Rd. ST2—3K 23
Club St. ST4—1D 28
Clumber Av. ST5—1K 27
Clumber Gro. ST5—2K 27
Cluny Pl. ST2—1K 23
Clyde Av. ST8—2C 6
Clyde Pl. ST5—3H 27
Clyde Rd. ST6—6J 17
Clyde St. ST1—3E 22
Clyde Wlk. ST1—3E 22
(off Clyde St.)
Clynes Way. ST3—4G 31
Coalpit Hill. ST7—5K 9
Coalville Pl. ST3—2G 31
Coates Pl. ST6—4K 11
Cobden St. ST3—6A 30
Cobden St. ST5—7F 17
Cobham Pl. ST3—7F 31
Cob Moor Rd. ST7—7C 4
Cobridge Rd. ST1—2D 22
Cocknage Rd. ST3
—6A 30 to 4D 34
Cocks La. ST9—2G 19
Cockster Rd. ST3—4J 29
Colclough Av. ST5—5C 16
Colclough La. ST6—5F 11
Colclough Rd. ST3—6G 31
Coleridge Rd. ST3—5J 29
Cole St. ST8—4A 6
Colin Cres. ST3—3G 31
Colindene Gro. ST4—1D 28
Collard Av. ST5—3J 21
College Rd. ST1 & ST4—4E 22
College Rd. ST7—6B 2
Colley Rd. ST6—6H 11
Colliers Way. ST8—3A 6
Collingwood Gro. ST4—6B 22
Collin Rd. ST4—3B 28
Collinson Rd. ST6—5F 11
Collis Av. ST4—5A 22
Columbine Wlk. ST6—2F 17
(off Ladywell Rd.)
Colville St. ST4—1J 29
Colwyn Dri. ST8—6B 6
Combe Dri. ST3—3F 35
Comfrey Clo. ST3—2F 35
Commerce St. ST3—4B 30
Commercial Rd. ST1—3G 23
Commercial St. ST6—6J 17
Common La. ST3—4D 34
Community Dri. ST6—4B 18
Como Pl. ST5—1F 27
Compton St. ST1—3E 22
Conewood Pl. ST3—6H 29
Conford Clo. ST2—4J 23
Congleton Rd. CW12 & ST7
—1A 4
Congleton Rd. ST7—3G 5
(Biddulph)
Congleton Rd. ST7—4K 9
(Talke)
Congleton Rd. ST8—3B 6
Congleton Rd. N. ST7—1K 9
Congleton Rd. S. ST7—1K 9
Congreve Rd. ST3—5J 29
Conifer Gro. ST3—5J 29
Conifers, The. ST7—1B 8
Coniston Gro. ST5—3J 27
Coniston Pl. ST4—1C 32
Connaught St. ST6—3F 17
Conrad Clo. ST3—4C 30
Consall Gro. ST4—2F 22
Consett Rd. ST3—7J 29
Consort St. ST4—7E 22
Constable Av. ST5—7A 16
Constance Av. ST4—7E 28
Convent Clo. ST4—6C 22
Convent St. ST4—6D 22
Conway Rd. ST8—5A 6
Conway St. ST4—6F 23

Cooke St. ST3—4A 30
Cookson Av. ST3—6B 30
Coolidge St. ST6—2F 17
Cooper Av. ST5—4B 22
Cooper St. ST1—4E 22
Cooper St. ST5—7A 16
Coopers Way. ST8—3K 5
Copeland Av. ST5—4J 27
Copeland Av. ST12—7D 32
Copeland St. ST4—6E 22
Cope's Av. ST6—1G 17
Cope St. ST2—4E 18
Coppice Av. ST5—5B 20
Coppice Clo. ST8—4B 6
Coppice Rd. ST7—4J 9
Coppice, The. ST6—6A 18
Coppice View. ST5—2H 21
Copp La. ST6—3E 16
Copplestone Gro. ST3—4D 30
Coppull Pl. ST6—5J 11
Coral Gro. ST4—1E 32
Corbett Wlk. ST6—2F 17
(off Ladywell Rd.)
Corby Pl. ST3—4K 29
Coree Grn. ST3—2B 30
Corfield Pl. ST6—7B 12
Corina Way. ST3—3C 30
Corinth Way. ST6—2F 17
Cornelious St. ST3—6F 31
Cornes St. ST1—4G 23
Corneville Rd. ST2—3A 24
Cornfield Rd. ST8—4B 6
Cornhill Clo. ST5—4K 15
Cornhill Rd. ST6—7A 12
Cornwall Av. ST5—3K 27
Cornwall St. ST4—1E 28
Cornwall St. ST3—3B 30
Cornwell Rd. ST3—4A 30
Cornwood Gro. ST3—7D 30
Coronation Av. ST3—4A 30
Coronation Av. ST7—1A 8
Coronation Av. ST8—6K 5
Coronation Cres. ST7—3A 10
Coronation Rd. ST4—6B 22
Coronation Rd. ST5—6K 21
Coronation St. ST6—1G 17
Corporation St. ST4—1D 28
Corporation St. ST5—5J 21
Corwell Rd. ST3—4A 30
Coseley St. ST6—4A 18
Cotehill Rd. ST9—3G 25
Cotesheath St. ST1—5G 23
Coton Rise. ST12—7H 33
Cotswold Av. ST5—3F 21
Cotswold Cres. ST2—4E 18
Cottage La. ST8—3E 6
Cottages, The. ST6—6F 25
Cotterill Gro. ST6—6F 17
Cotton Rd. ST6—6E 10
Cottons Row. ST4—6A 22
Cottonwood Gro. ST7—1G 11
Coupe Dri. ST3—2F 31
Court La. ST3—2J 21
Courtney Pl. ST3—7D 30
Court Number 1. ST3—5D 30
Courtway Dri. ST1—5B 18
Coverdale Clo. ST4—1F 35
Coverley Pl. ST4—1C 28
Covert Gdns. ST7—4K 9
Covert, The. ST5—7C 20
(Keele)
Covert, The. ST5—5K 27
(Northwood)
Cowallmoor La. ST13—7F 7
Cowen St. ST6—6B 12
Cowley Way. ST2—7D 24
Cowlishaw Clo. ST8—6J 5
Cowlishaw Rd. ST6—6K 11
Cowper St. ST1—4J 29
Coyney Gro. ST3—4F 31
Crabtree Av. ST8—4A 6
Crabtree Clo. ST4—6J 23
Crackley Bank. ST5—3A 16
Crackley La. ST5—3A 20
Craigside. ST8—3A 6
Craig Wlk. ST7—2F 9
Cranberry La. ST7—7A 2
Cranberry Moss La. ST7—1A 8
Cranbourne Av. ST2—3F 19
Cranbrook Clo. ST4—1D 32
Crane St. ST1—7K 17

Cranfield Dri. ST7—1A 8
Cranfield Pl. ST2—4A 24
Cranford M. ST7—1A 8
Cranford Way. ST2—3C 24
Cranleigh Av. ST1—5B 18
Cranmer St. ST4—7E 22
Cranswick Gro. ST2—5C 24
Cranwell Pl. ST3—7E 30
Cranworth Gro. ST3—7D 30
Craven Clo. ST4—7F 23
Crawford St. ST4—2G 29
Crediton Av. ST6—1A 18
Crescent Gro. ST4—5B 22
Crescent, The. ST3—3G 31
Crescent, The. ST4—3B 28
Crescent, The. ST5—1H 27
(Newcastle)
Crescent, The. ST5—4C 20
(Silverdale)
Cresswell La. ST11—7E 36
Cresswell Old La. ST11—7E 36
Cresswell Rd. ST1—3H 23
Cresswellshawe Rd. ST7—6D 2
Crestbrook Rd. ST2—6F 19
Crestfield Rd. ST3—7E 30
Crestway Rd. ST2—3G 19
Crewe Rd. ST7—2A 8
(Alsager)
Crewe Rd. ST7—7F 3
(Church Lawton)
Crick Rd. ST1—4H 23
Critchlow Gro. ST3—6J 29
Croft Av. ST5—7D 16
Croft Ct. ST6—4A 18
Croft Cres. ST4—1D 28
Crofters Clo. ST8—3K 5
Croftfield St. ST2—6C 24
Croft Rd. ST5—4J 21
Croft St. ST6—5H 17
Croft, The. ST4—2C 28
Cromartie St. ST3—5B 30
(in two parts)
Cromer Cres. ST1—2H 23
Cromer Rd. ST1—2H 23
Cromer St. ST5—2A 22
Crompton Gro. ST4—3F 33
Cromwell St. ST1—7B 18
Cromwell St. ST8—2A 6
Crosby Rd. ST4—4B 28
Crossdale Av. ST2—3E 18
Cross Edge. ST6—5F 13
Crossfield Av. ST8—5A 6
Crossfield Av. ST11—5A 36
Cross Hill. ST6—5H 17
Crossland Pl. E. ST3—7F 31
Crossland Pl. W. ST3—6F 31
Cross La. ST7—1D 14
Crossley Rd. ST3—2J 17
Cross May St. ST5—6H 21
Crossmeade Gro. ST1—7D 18
Cross St. ST3—2G 31
Cross St. ST5—5K 15
(Chesterton)
Cross St. ST5—5E 16
(Longbridge Hayes)
Cross St. ST7—1C 8
Cross St. ST8—3A 6
Crossway Rd. ST6—6A 18
Crossway Rd. ST7—7G 3
Crossways. ST8—2C 6
Crossway, The. ST5—3K 21
Croston St. ST1—4E 22
Crouch Av. ST6—1J 17
Crowborough Rd. ST8 & ST13
—5D 6
Crowcrofts Rd. ST4—1H 33
Crown Bank. ST1—2F 23
Crown Bank. ST7—5K 9
Crown Bank Cres. ST7—6K 9
Crown St. ST1—3F 23
Crown St. ST5—5D 20
Crowther St. ST4—6F 23
Croxden Rd. ST2—7F 19
Croyde Pl. ST3—2F 35
Crystal St. ST6—7K 17
Cumberbatch Av. ST6—5K 11
Cumberland Clo. ST7—5A 10
Cumberland St. ST4—1H 29
Cumberland St. ST5—6A 22
Cumbria Ho. ST5—2K 27
Cumming St. ST4—5B 22

Curland Pl. ST3—5E 30
Curtis St. ST3—2H 35
Curzon Av. ST7—6D 2
Curzon Rd. ST6—3J 17
Curzon St. ST5—4A 22
Cutts St. ST1—4E 22
Cynthia Gro. ST6—3J 17
Cypress Gro. ST5—5K 15
Cypress Gro. ST11—5B 36

Dace Gro. ST6—2K 17
Dahlia Clo. ST3—1G 31
Dain Pl. ST5—7D 16
Daintry St. ST4—3C 28
Dairylands Rd. ST7—7G 3
Daisy Bank. ST7—7A 2
Daisy Pl. ST4—3H 29
Dale Av. ST6—6B 12
Dalecot Grn. ST2—6C 24
Dalegarth Gro. ST3—7D 30
Dalehall Gdns. ST6—5G 17
Dalehead Ct. ST3—7E 30
Dales Clo. ST8—3F 7
Dales Grn. Rd. ST7—6E 4
Dale St. ST6—5G 17
Dale View. ST3—4G 31
Daleview Dri. ST5—5D 20
Dalton Gro. ST2—5C 24
Daly Cres. ST5—5C 20
Dam La. ST1—1E 6
Danebower Rd. ST4—3E 32
Danebridge Gro. ST1—1J 23
Dane Clo. ST7—1A 8
Dane Dri. ST8—2C 6
Dane Gdns. ST7—2E 10
Danehill Gro. ST4—6C 28
Danemead Clo. ST3—1F 35
Danes Croft. ST4—1E 32
Dane Wlk. ST1—2G 23
Darnley St. ST4—6F 23
Darrall Gdns. ST4—4B 28
Darsham Gdns. ST5—5K 27
Dart Av. ST6—1J 17
Dart Clo. ST7—7A 2
Dartford Pl. ST6—1A 18
Dart Gro. ST8—2B 6
Dartmouth Av. ST5—1H 27
Dartmouth Pl. ST3—7E 30
Dartmouth St. ST6—4K 17
Dart Pl. ST5—3H 27
Dash Gro. ST6—4A 18
Davenport St. ST6—5F 17
Daventry Clo. ST2—4J 23
David Rd. ST3—6E 30
Davis Clo. ST7—7E 2
Davison St. ST6—6J 17
Davis St. ST4—4D 22
Davy Clo. ST2—3K 23
Dawlish Dri. ST2—4A 24
Dawn Av. ST6—1J 17
Dawn View. ST3—4G 31
Dayson Pl. ST5—6D 16
Deakin Gro. ST5—2K 27
Deakin Rd. ST6—6K 11
Dean Clo. ST8—3C 6
Dean Hollow. ST7—3D 14
Dean Pl. ST1—4G 23
Deansberry Clo. ST4—7D 28
Deanscroft Way. ST3—3C 30
Deansgate. ST5—6H 21
Dean's La. ST5—3J 15
Dean St. ST2—2B 24
Deans Way. ST4—2E 32
Deaville Rd. ST2—3B 24
Debenham Cres. ST2—4J 23
Dee Clo. ST7—5A 10
Dee Clo. ST8—2C 6
Dee La. ST5—3H 27
Deepdale Clo. ST6—3D 18
Defoe Dri. ST3—2D 30
Delamere Gro. ST4—1D 32
Delamere Gro. ST5—4K 21
Delaney Dri. ST3—3E 30
Delius Gro. ST1—1J 23
Dell, The. ST5—5D 20
Dellwood Gro. ST3—1C 30
Delphside. ST7—3F 15
Delph Wlk. ST4—1J 29
Delves Pl. ST5—2J 27

Denbigh Clo. ST5—3A 28
Denbigh Clo. ST8—5A 6
Denbigh St. ST1—1E 22
Denby Av. ST3—2A 30
Dency Gro. ST6—2J 17
Denehurst Clo. ST3—5F 31
Dene Side. ST5—6H 21
Denewood Pl. ST3—6G 31
Denford ST7—5D 2
Denham Sq. ST3—6H 29
Denmark Ho. ST4—2J 29
Dennington Cres. ST3—6H 29
Dennis Round Ct. ST7—1C 8
Dennis St. ST4—2J 29
Denry Cres. ST5—6C 16
Denshaw Wlk. ST3—3B 30
(off Forrister St.)
Denstone Cres. ST3—5J 29
Dentdale Clo. ST3—1F 35
Denton St. ST5—4J 27
Denton Gro. ST3—4D 30
Derby Pl. ST5—3K 27
Derby Rd. ST7—5K 9
Derby St. ST1—1G 23
Derby St. ST4—3H 29
Dereham Way. ST2—5C 24
Derek Dri. ST1—7C 18
Derwent Clo. ST7—7A 2
Derwent Cres. ST7—2E 10
Derwent Dri. ST8—2C 6
Derwent Pl. ST5—3H 21
Derwent St. ST1—1E 22
Devana Wlk. ST3—5H 31
Devon Clo. ST5—3K 27
Devon Gro. ST8—2A 6
Devonshire Sq. ST2—5B 24
Dewsbury Rd. ST4—7H 23
Diamond Clo. ST3—3F 35
Diamond Clo. ST8—3A 6
Diamond Clo. ST12—7F 33
Diamond Ridge. ST12—7F 33
Diana Rd. ST1—7D 18
Diarmid Rd. ST4—6C 28
Dibden Ct. ST4—7D 22
Dickenson Rd. E. ST6—6A 18
Dickenson Rd. W. ST6—6A 18
Dickens St. ST2—2B 24
Dickson Ho. ST1—4G 23
Diglake St. ST7—2F 15
Dilhorne Gro. ST3—6B 30
Dilhorne La. ST11 & ST10
—4K 31
Dilhorne Rd. ST11 & ST10
—3C 36
Dilke St. ST1—1G 23
Dill Gro. ST3—2G 35
Dimmelow St. ST3—2G 31
Dimsdale Pde. E. ST5—6J 17
Dimsdale Pde. W. ST5—7C 16
Dimsdale St. ST6—6G 17
Dimsdale View. ST5—7B 16
Dimsdale View E. ST5—7D 16
Dimsdale View W. ST5—7D 16
Dingle, The. ST6—5F 13
Dividy Rd. ST2—3J 23 to 1D 30
Dixon's Row. ST5—6K 15
Dobell Gro. ST3—3C 30
Dobson St. ST6—6A 18
Doctors Clo. ST8—3A 6
Doddington Pl. ST5—1J 27
Dogcroft Rd. ST6—7A 12
Dolespring Clo. ST11—3B 36
Dolly's La. ST6—3J 17
Dominic St. ST4—6D 22
Donald Rd. ST1—7C 18
Don Bates Ho. ST4—1C 28
Doncaster La. ST4—7C 22
Dorcas Dri. ST3—3J 29
Dorchester Wlk. ST2—4B 24
Doris Robinson Ct. ST3—1E 34
Dorking St. ST2—4J 23
Dorlan Clo. ST9—2G 19
Dorridge Gro. ST5—2B 22
Dorrington Clo. ST2—4E 18
Dorrington Gro. ST5—7E 16
Dorset Clo. ST2—3B 24
Dorset Dri. ST8—3A 6
Dorset Pl. ST5—3A 28
Dorset Pl. ST7—1C 10
Douglas Av. ST4—2C & 3C 28

Douglas Av. ST8—4A 6
Douglas Pl. ST1—4H 23
Douglas Rd. ST5—3H & 4H 21
Douglas St. ST1—7K 17
Doulton St. ST6—5J 17
Dovebank Gro. ST3—2F 35
Dovecote Pl. ST3—7D 30
Dovedale Clo. ST6—5D 10
Dovedale Pl. ST5—5B 20
Dove Gro. ST8—2B 6
Dove Pl. ST5—4H 27
Doveridge St. ST4—2G 29
Dove Rd. ST11—4B 36
Dover St. ST1—1G 23
Downey St. ST1—3F 23
Downfield Pl. ST2—4D 18
Downham Rd. ST5—4F 21
Downing Av. ST5—3A 22
Downsview Gro. ST3—4J 29
Dragon Sq. ST5—5A 16
Drake Clo. ST2—5J 23
Drakeford Ct. ST6—1C 18
Drakeford Gro. ST6—1C 18
Draw-well La. ST9—2H 25
Draycott Dri. ST5—3K 15
Draycott Old Rd. ST11—4C 36
Drayton Grn. ST2—4K 23
Drayton Rd. ST3—3A 30
Drayton St. ST5—6H 21
Drenfell Rd. ST7—4B 4
Dresden St. ST1—3G 23
Dreys, The. ST4—1E 32
Driffield Clo. ST2—5D 24
Drive, The. ST5 & ST7—7F 15
Droitwich Clo. ST5—4A 20
Drubbery La. ST3—6J 29
Drumber La. ST7—3D 4
Drumburn Clo. ST6—5G 11
Drummond St. ST6—5F 11
Dryberg Way. ST2—2K 23
Dryden Rd. ST6—7J 17
Ducal St. ST6—5G 17
Duddell Rd. ST6—3A 18
Dudley Pl. ST3—7F 31
Duesbury Grn. ST3—4K 29
Duke Bank Ter. ST6—1D 18
Duke Pl. ST5—5D 20
Duke St. ST4—3H 29
Duke St. ST5—7K 21
Duke St. ST8—4B 6
Dulverton Av. ST5—2H 27
Duncalf Gro. ST5—6D 16
Duncalf St. ST6—5G 17
Duncan St. ST4—1H 29
Dundas St. ST1—1G 23
Dundee Rd. ST1—3D 22
Dundee St. ST3—5A 30
Dunham Clo. ST1—7C 18
Dunkirk. ST5—5H 21
Dunkirk Ct. ST5—5H 21
Dunning St. ST6—1F 17
Dunnocksfold Rd. ST7—7A 2
Dunnockswood. ST7—7A 2
Dunrobin St. ST3—5B 30
Dunsany Gro. ST1—7C 18
Dunsford Av. ST2—3E 18
Dunster Rd. ST2—4A 30
Dunwood Dri. ST6—2J 17
Dunwood Dri. ST7—5D 2
Durber Clo. ST4—4D 18
Durber Clo. ST7—4D 14
Durham Gro. ST5—3A 28
Durston Pl. ST3—4E 30
Dyke St. ST1—2G 23
Dylan Rd. ST3—4C 30

Eagle St. ST1—2H 23
Eamont Av. ST6—1J 17
Eardleyend Rd. ST7—6D 8
Eardley St. ST4—1C 28
Earlsbrook Dri. ST4—1F 33
Earls Ct. ST5—5A 22
Earl's Dri. ST5—2J 27
Earls Rd. ST4—1E 32
Earl St. ST5—5A 22
(Newcastle)
Earl St. ST5—5D 20
(Silverdale)
Earlswood Rd. ST1—7E 18
Easdale Pl. ST5—2J 27

Easedale Clo. ST2—3E 18
Easedale Pl. ST5—2J 27
E. Bank Ride. ST11—3B 36
Eastbank Rd. ST1—1E 22
Eastbourne Rd. ST1—2G 23
Eastbridge Av. ST1—5B 18
East Ct. ST7—6E 2
East Cres. ST1—5C 18
East Cres. ST5—3A 22
Eastdean Av. ST2—4K 23
East Dri. ST8—3B 6
Easters Gro. ST2—4F 19
East Gro. ST3—6F 31
Easthead Wlk. ST1—3E 22
East Precinct. ST1—2F 23
East St. ST3—2G 31
East Ter. ST6—6K 11
East View. ST6—6H 17
Eastwick Cres. ST4—7D 28
Eastwood Av. ST6—1J 17
Eastwood Pl. ST1—3F 23
Eastwood Rd. ST1—3G 23
Eaton Rd. ST7—7C 2
Eaton St. ST1—2G 23
Eaves La. ST2—2B 24
Eaveswood Rd. ST2—7G 19
Ebor St. ST3—5C 30
Ebury Gro. ST3—6E 30
Ecclestone Pl. ST6—6J 11
Edale Clo. ST5—5C 20
Edale Clo. ST6—5D 10
Eddisbury Dri. ST5—3K 15
Eden Clo. ST2—2D 10
Eden Clo. ST8—2C 6
Eden Gro. ST3—6E 30
Edenhurst Av. ST3—6G 31
Edensor Ct. ST5—6A 16
Edensor Rd. ST3—5A 30
Edensor St. ST5—6A 16
Edensor Ter. ST3—5A 30
Edgar Pl. ST3—1B 30
Edge Av. ST6—6J 11
Edge Ct. ST8—4A 6
Edgefield Rd. ST3—2B 30
Edgefields La. ST9—6G 13
Edge La. ST9—5H 13
Edgeley Rd. ST8—4B 6
Edge St. ST6—3H 17
Edgeview Clo. ST2—3G 19
Edgeview Rd. ST2—2G 19
Edgware St. ST1—1E 22
Edison St. ST4—1G 29
Edmonton Gro. ST2—4D 18
Ednam Pl. ST3—6F 31
Edwal Rd. ST3—2F 31
Edward Av. ST4—1E 32
Edward Av. ST5—1J 27
Edward Davies Rd. ST6—3A 18
Edward St. ST4—7H 23
Edward St. ST5—2A 22
Edward St. ST7—2F 15
Edwards Way. ST7—7E 2
Egerton Rd. ST4—6B 22
Egerton St. ST1—5G 23
Elaine Av. ST6—4K 17
Elburton Rd. ST4—1K 29
Elder Pl. ST6—6J 17
Elder St. ST6—6K & 7K 17
Eldon St. ST1—7B 18
Eleanor Cres. ST5—1H 27
Eleanor Pl. ST5—1H 27
Eleanor View. ST5—1J 27
Elenora St. ST4—7E 22
Elers Gro. ST6—6G 17
Elgar Cres. ST1—1K 23
Elgin St. ST4—5E 22
Elgood La. ST6—5E 10
Eliases La. ST8—1E 6
Elisabeth Ct. ST4—6C 22
Elizabeth Ct. ST7—6K 9
Elizabeth Dri. ST5—6A 16
Elizabeth St. ST1—2H 23
Elkstone Clo. ST6—1G 17
Ellam's Pl. ST5—5F 21
Ellastone Gro. ST4—1C 28
Elldawn Av. ST6—3D 18
Ellerby Rd. ST3—7H 29
Ellestree Gro. ST1—7E 18
Ellgreave St. ST6—5G 17
Ellington Clo. ST2—4K 23
Elliot Dri. ST9—2G 25

Elliot Rd. ST4—1J 29
Elliott St. ST5—5A 22
Ellison St. ST5—1A 22
Ellis St. ST6—6A 18
Elmbrook Clo. ST3—7E 30
Elm Clo. ST7—4D 10
Elmcroft Rd. ST2—7F 19
Elmdon Pl. ST3—1G 35
Elm Gro. ST7—7E 2
Elmhurst. ST5—3G 27
Elmhurst Clo. ST2—4J 23
Elm Pl. ST3—6J 29
Elmsmere Av. ST3—6K 29
Elmsmere Rd. ST2—7F 19
Elmstead Clo. ST4—6C 28
Elms, The. ST5—6E 16
Elm St. ST5—4A 22
Elm St. ST6—6J 17
Elms Way. ST3—5F 31
Elm Tree Dri. ST7—4F 15
Elmwood Clo. ST7—7G 3
Elmwood Clo. ST11—5B 36
Elmwood Dri. ST11—5B 36
Elphinstone Rd. ST4—4C 28
Elsby Pl. ST6—6J 11
Elsby Rd. ST7—2F 9
Elsing St. ST4—1G 29
Elstree Clo. ST3—5E 30
Elswick Rd. ST4—6H 23
Eltham Gdns. ST5—2A 22
Elton Ter. ST6—5F 11
Ely Wlk. ST3—3B 30
Embers Way. ST9—4K 13
Emberton St. ST5—6A 16
  (Chesterton)
Emberton St. ST5—1K 21
  (Wolstanton)
Embleton Wlk. ST6—6G 17
Emerson Rd. ST6—7J 17
Emery Av. ST1—5C 18
Emery Av. ST5—7G 21
Emery St. ST6—7K 17
Empire Pas. ST4—1D 28
Empire St. ST4—1D 28
Emsworth Rd. ST3—7H 29
Enderley St. ST5—4J 21
Endon Dri. ST8—6K 5
Endon Rd. ST6—1C 18
Englesea Av. ST3—2F 31
Ennerdale Clo. ST6—5G 17
Enoch St. ST6—6H 17
Enstone Clo. ST3—7J 29
Enstone Ct. ST5—4J 27
Enterprise Cen. ST1—4D 22
Ephraim St. ST1—4G 23
Epping Rd. ST4—4B 28
Epworth St. ST4—7D 22
Ernest Pl. ST1—1H 29
Eros Cres. ST1—7C 18
Erill Clo. ST4—1F 29
Erskine St. ST3—6B 30
Eskdale Pl. ST4—1D 32
Esk Way. ST5—3J 27
Esperanto Way. ST6—5A 18
Essex Dri. ST8—2B 10
Essex Dri. ST8—1B 6
Essex Pl. ST5—1H 27
Eton Av. ST5—3G 27
Etruria Old Rd. ST1—3C 22
Etruria Rd. ST5, ST4 & ST1
  —4A 22
Etruria Trading Est. ST4
  —3B 22
Etruria Vale Rd. ST1—3D 22
Etruria Way. ST4—3B 22
Etruscan St. ST1—4C 22
Etruscan Wlk. ST12—4J 33
Eva Gro. ST5—7A 28
Evans St. ST4—4H 17
Evelyn St. ST4—2H 29
Everest Rd. ST7—1D 10
Eversley Rd. ST3—5D 30
Evesham Way. ST3—4D 30
Exeter Grn. ST2—4B 24
Exmouth Gro. ST6—6J 17
Eyre St. ST6—6G 17

Faceby Gro. ST3—1H 35
Fairbank Av. ST4—2C 28
Fairclough Pl. ST6—2J 17

Fairfax St. ST1—7B 18
Fairfield Av. ST3—7B 30
Fairfield Av. ST5—2K 21
Fairfield Av. ST6—5F 13
Fairfields. ST7—3F 15
Fairfields Rd. ST8—2F 7
Fairhaven Gro. ST1—7C 18
Fairlawn Clo. ST3—7D 30
Fairlawns. ST5—4J 21
Fairlight Gro. ST3—2F 35
Fairoak. ST5—3G 27
Fairview Av. ST7—7D 2
Fairway. ST4—7B 28
Fairway Rd. ST6—2J 17
Fairway, The. ST7—7C 2
Falcon Rd. ST3—1F 35
Falkirk Grange. ST5—7G 21
Fallowfield. ST3—7J 29
Fanny's Croft. ST7—2D 8
Faraday Pl. ST4—7B 22
Farams Rd. ST4—4E 2
Farcroft Av. ST5—7B 16
Fareham Gro. ST3—1D 34
Far Green Ind. Est. ST1—1G 23
Farington Pl. ST6—6J 11
Farland Gro. ST6—6J 11
Farleigh Gro. ST2—5B 24
Farmadine. ST4—1E 32
Farman Clo. ST3—1H 35
Farmers Bank. ST5—5D 20
Farmer St. ST3—5B 30
Farmside La. ST8—2F 7
Farnwood Clo. ST6—6G 31
Farnborough Dri. ST3—1H 35
Farndale St. ST6—2F 17
Farne Gro. ST3—4K 29
Farnham Dri. ST8—6K 5
Farnworth Wlk. ST6—6G 17
Farnworth Rd. ST3—4D 30
Farrington Clo. ST6—2C 18
Faulkner Pl. ST3—3E 30
Fawcett Way. ST1—1G 23
  (off Plough St.)
Fawfield Dri. ST6—6E 10
Fearns Av. ST5—4C 16
Fearson Grn. ST6—2C 18
Featherstone Gro. ST4—7D 22
Federation Rd. ST6—4G 17
Fegg Hayes Rd. ST6—6J 11
Felcourt Gdns. ST1—1H 23
Fellbrook Ct. ST2—2K 23
Fellbrook La. ST2—2K 23
Fellgate Ct. ST5—5J 21
Fell St. ST6—4A 18
Felstead St. ST2—2F 19
Fenlow Av. ST2—4J 23
Fennel Gro. ST3—2G 35
Fenpark Ind. Est. ST1—2K 29
Fenpark Rd. ST4—1J 29
Fenton Ind. Est. ST4—6J 23
Fenton Pk. ST4—1K 29
Fenton Rd. ST2—5H 23
Fenton Wlk. ST3—1H 33
Fermain Clo. ST5—4G 27
Ferncroft Clo. ST4—1E 32
Ferndale Clo. ST9—2F 25
Ferndale Clo. ST11—5A 36
Ferndown Clo. ST3—6C 30
Ferndown Dri. ST5—5K 27
Ferndown Dri. S. ST5—6K 27
Ferney Pl. ST6—6E 10
Fernhurst Gro. ST3—7D 30
Fernlea Cres. ST9—4K 13
Fernleaf Clo. ST7—3F 3
Fernlea Gro. ST3—2F 31
  (Longton)
Fernlea Gro. ST3—4F 35
  (Meir Heath)
Fern Pl. ST3—5A 30
Fernwood Grn. ST4—1F 33
Ferrand Clo. ST4—5D 28
Festing St. ST1—1G 23
Festival Way. ST1—2C 22
Fiddlers Bank. ST4—4F 13
Field Av. ST2—3F 19
Field Clo. ST11—2A 24
Fielden Clo. ST6—3D 18
Field End Clo. ST4—2E 32
Fielding St. ST4—2E 28
Field Pl. ST3—2B 30
Fields Clo. ST7—7E 2

Fields Rd. ST7—1E 8
Field View. ST3—3G 31
Field View. ST8—2B 6
Fieldway. ST2—3E 24
Fieldway. ST3—4H 29
Field Way. ST7—7E 2
Fieldway. ST11—1J 35
Fieldway, The. ST4—1B 32
Fife St. ST4—3K 29
Fifth Av. ST7—3A 10
Filey Clo. ST2—4C 24
Finchdean Clo. ST3—1F 35
Finch Pl. ST8—2K 11
Finchsmith Pl. ST3—5A 30
Finch St. ST8—3A 12
Finney Grn. ST2—3K 23
Finstock Av. ST3—7H 29
Firbank Pl. ST3—3E 30
First Av. ST3—2C 24
First Av. ST5—6E 16
First Av. ST7—3A 10
Fir Tree Pl. ST5—5A 16
Fir Tree Rd. ST3—7D 30
Firwood Rd. ST8—2D 6
Fisher St. ST8—2K 11
Fishpond Way. ST2—6E 18
Fistral Clo. ST3—3C 30
Fitzgerald Clo. ST3—3G 31
Fitzherbert Rd. ST1—5C 18
Five Oaks Clo. ST5—4F 27
Flackett St. ST3—2B 30
Flamborough Gro. ST6—6G 17
Flash La. ST2—3G 19
Flash La. ST4—4B 28
Flatts Rd. ST6—7C 12
Flaxman Clo. ST12—4H 33
Flax St. ST4—1E 28
Fleckney Av. ST3—4D 30
Fleming Rd. ST4—7E 22
Fletcher Bank. ST5—5H 21
Fletcher Cres. ST2—3F 19
Fletcher Rd. ST4—2D 28
Fletcher St. ST1—4E 22
Fleur Gro. ST4—1A 30
Flintsham Gro. ST1—1F 23
Flint St. ST3—2G 31
Floral St. ST4—6E 22
Florence Rd. ST4—6C 28
Florence St. ST5—5J 21
Florida Clo. ST6—5K 17
Floyd St. ST4—6E 22
Foden Av. ST7—1G 9
Foden St. ST4—2D 28
Fogg St. ST5—5J 21
Fogg St. E. ST5—5J 21
Fogg St. W. ST5—5J 21
Foley Pl. ST4—3K 29
Foley Rd. ST3—4K 29
Foley St. ST4—3A 30
Folly Cotts. ST8—2G 7
Fontaine Pl. ST4—2D 28
Fonthill Wlk. ST2—2K 23
Forber Rd. ST4—3C 28
Ford Av. ST6—7K 11
Ford Grn. Rd. ST6—4A 18
Ford Hayes La. ST2 & ST3
  —6C 24
Fords La. ST7—5F 5
Ford St. ST4—5B 22
Ford St. ST5—4C 20
Forest Clo. ST5—3F 27
Forest Ct. ST1—1F 23
  (off Union St.)
Forest St. ST3—1E 34
Forestside Gro. ST4—5C 28
Forge La. ST1—3C 22
Forge Side. ST9—4K 13
Forge Way Ind. Est. ST8—7K 5
Forrester Gro. ST8—3A 6
Forresters Bank. ST2—2G 19
Forrister St. ST3—3B 30
Forster St. ST6—2F 17
Forsyte Rd. ST3—1A 30
Forum Rd. ST5—1E 20
Fosbrook Pl. ST4—6A 22
Foster Ct. ST3—4J 29
Foundry La. ST2—4A 24
Foundry La. ST8—4B 4
Foundry Sq. ST6—7D 12
Foundry St. ST1—2F 23
Fountain Ct. ST8—2B 6
Fountain Pl. ST6—5H 17

Fountains Av. ST5—2J 27
Fountain Sq. ST1—2F 23
Fountain St. ST4—1H 29
Fourth Av. ST2—2D 24
Fourth Av. ST7—3B 10
Fowler's La. ST2—3H 19
Foxfield Way. ST3—7J 29
Fox Gdns. ST7—4K 9
Foxglove Clo. ST3—2G 31
Foxglove La. ST5—5K 27
Fox Gro. ST5—5K 27
Foxlands Clo. ST3—2C 24
Foxley La. ST2—4D 18
Frampton Gro. ST6—6G 11
Francis St. ST6—7H 11
Franklin Rd. ST4—7C 22
Franklyn St. ST1—4G 23
Frank St. ST4—1D 28
Fraser St. ST6—6K 17
Freckleton Pl. ST3—1H 35
Frederick Av. ST4—7D 22
Frederick St. ST4—1H 29
Freebridge Clo. ST3—3D 30
Freedom Dri. ST7—1G 11
Freehold St. ST5—6K 21
Free Trade St. ST1—1G 23
Fremantle Rd. ST4—3C 28
Frenchmoor Gro. ST3—6D 30
Freshwater Gro. ST2—3J 23
Friars Pl. ST2—6F 19
Friars Rd. ST2—6F 19
Friars St. ST5—6J 21
Friar St. ST3—3B 30
Friars Wlk. ST5—1J 27
Friarswood Rd. ST5—6J 21
Frobisher St. ST6—7E 12
Frodingham Rd. ST2—5C 24
Froghall. ST5—5J 21
Frome Wlk. ST6—1J 17
Frozer Ho. ST3—7E 30
Fulford Dale. ST11—6G 35
Fulford Rd. ST11—7K 35
Fuller St. ST6—1G 17
Fullwood Wlk. ST2—5B 24
Fulmar Pl. ST3—1G 35
Furlong La. ST6—6G 17
Furlong Pde. ST6—5H 17
Furlong St. ST6—5H 17
Furlong Rd. ST6—1G 17
Furnace Rd. ST3—5C 30
Furnival St. ST6—7K 17

Gables, The. ST7—7C 2
Gable St. ST4—1E 28
Gainsborough Rd. ST3—7H 29
Gainsborough Rd. ST5—7A 16
Galleys Bank. ST7—1D 10
Galloway Rd. ST2—6D 24
Gallowstree La. ST5—7F 21
Galsworthy Rd. ST3—1A 30
Garbett St. ST6—5E 10
Gardeners Clo. ST8—6K 5
Gardenholm Clo. ST3—7E 30
Garden Pl. ST4—6B 22
Garden St. ST4—1C 28
Garden St. ST5—6K 21
Gardiner Dri. ST3—5K 29
Garfield Av. ST4—6C 28
Garfield Ct. ST4—6C 28
Garfield Cres. ST4—6C 28
Garfield St. ST1—4E 22
Garibaldi St. ST1—3C 22
Garlick St. ST6—4A 18
Garner St. ST4—4C & 5C 22
Garner St. ST1—3D 22
Garnett Rd. E. ST5—1J 21
Garnett Rd. W. ST5—7D 16
Garnham Pl. ST3—4A 30
Garsdale Cres. ST3—7H 29
Garth St. ST1—2G 23
Gaskell Rd. ST2—3C 24
Gate St. ST3—2G 31
Gate Way. ST5—3K 15
Gatley Gro. ST3—2G 35
Gawsworth Clo. ST3—1B 30
Gawsworth Clo. ST7—1C 8
Gayton Av. ST2—3F 19
Gedney Gro. ST5—5J 27
Geen St. ST4—7E 22
Gemini Gro. ST6—6H 11

Geneva Dri. ST1—7D 18
Geneva Dri. ST5—1F 27
Geoffrey Gro. ST3—3F 31
George Av. ST3—6G 31
George Bates Clo. ST7—1C 8
George Ct. ST3—4A 30
George St. ST4—7H 23
George St. ST5—6A 16
(Chesterton)
George St. ST5—5K 21
(Newcastle)
George St. ST5—4C 20
(Silverdale)
George St. ST5—7E 16
(Wolstanton)
George St. ST7—4D 14
Georges Way. ST7—3F 15
Gerrard St. ST4—6D 22
Gibbing St. ST1—1G 23
Gibson Gro. ST5—5K 15
Gibson Pl. ST3—5F 31
Gibson St. ST6—3G 17
Gifford Pl. ST4—1C 28
Gilbern Dri. ST8—6K 5
Gilbert Clo. ST7—2C 10
Gilbert St. ST6—5E 10
Gilchrist Pl. ST6—6J 17
Giles Wlk. ST1—1H 23
Gill Bank Rd. ST6—5D 10
Gill Bank Rd. ST7—4D 10
Gilliat Wlk. ST2—5B 24
Gill Wlk. ST1—3E 22
(off Yates La.)
Gilman Av. ST2—3F 19
Gilman Pl. ST1—2G 23
Gilman St. ST1—3G 23
Gimson St. ST4—1H 29
Girsby Clo. ST4—3F 33
Gitana St. ST1—2F 23
Glade, The. ST5—5H 27
Gladstone Gro. ST8—3C 6
Gladstone Pl. ST4—2C 28
Gladstone St. ST4—4B 22
Gladwyn St. ST2—2B 24
Glaisher Dri. ST3—1H 35
Glandore Rd. ST3—3E 30
Glass St. ST1—2F 23
Glastonbury Clo. ST9—2H 19
Glebe Clo. ST11—5B 36
Glebe Ct. ST4—7F 23
Glebedale Rd. ST4—1H 29
Glebe St. ST4—7E 22
Glebe St. ST7—2K 9
Glencastle Way. ST4—3F 33
Glencoe St. ST3—5A 30
Glendale Ct. ST5—5K 27
Glendale St. ST6—6J 17
Glendue gro. ST4—2F 33
Gleneagles Cres. ST1—7C 18
Glenfield Way. ST2—6D 24
Glenroyd Av. ST2—5K 23
Glenroyd Wlk. ST2—5B 24
Glenwood Clo. ST3—3A 30
Glenwood Clo. ST5—5D 20
Globe St. ST6—5G 17
Gloucester Grange. ST5—2K 27
Gloucester Rd. ST7—2B 10
Glover St. ST1—1G 23
Glyn Pl. ST6—2H 17
Goddard St. ST3—3B 30
Godfrey Rd. ST2—3A 24
Golborn Av. ST3—4F 35
Golborn Clo. ST3—4G 35
Goldcrest Way. ST8—3C 6
Goldenhill Rd. ST4—3A 30
Goldsmith Pl. ST3—3C 30
Gold St. ST3—4A 30
Golf Links Clo. ST6—5E 10
Goms Mill Rd. ST3—6K 29
(in two parts)
Goodfellow St. ST6—1F 17
Goodson St. ST1—2F 23
Goodwick Clo. ST4—3F 33
Goodwin Av. ST5—4J 21
Goodwin Rd. ST3—5G 31
Goodwood Pl. ST4—1E 32
Goosemoor Gro. ST3—1G 35
Goose St. ST5—6J 21
Gordon Av. ST6—6A 18
Gordon Ct. ST5—3F 21
Gordon Cres. ST1—6B 18

Gordon Rd. ST6—6E 10
Gordon St. ST5—3F 21
Gordon St. ST6—4K 17
Gorse St. ST4—3H 29
Gort Rd. ST5—2G 21
Gosforth Gro. ST3—1H 35
Govan Rd. ST4—6H 23
Gowan Av. ST6—1J 17
Gower St. ST3—4B 30
Gower St. ST5—5K 21
Gowy Clo. ST7—1A 8
Grafton Av. ST6—4K 17
Grafton Rd. ST3—3B 30
Grafton St. ST1—1G 23
Graham St. ST2—3K 23
Granby Wlk. ST4—1C 28
Granchester Clo. ST3—2G 35
Grange Ct. ST8—1B 6
Grange La. ST5—2A 22
Grange Rd. ST3—2E 34
Grange St. ST6—7K 17
Grange, The. ST3—5F 31
Grangewood Av. ST3—2E 34
Grangewood Rd. ST3—7F 31
Granstone Clo. ST6—5J 11
Grantham Pl. ST2—7E 18
Grantley Clo. ST3—6K 29
Grant St. ST4—7F 23
Granville Av. ST1—6B 18
Granville Av. ST5—5K 21
Granville Rd. ST2—2A 24
Granville St. ST1—1E 22
Granwood Rd. ST2—7D 32
Grasmere Av. ST5—3J 27
Grasmere Ter. ST6—2J 17
Grass Rd. ST6—7E 12
Grassygreen La. ST7—4D 14
Gratton La. ST9—3K 13
Gratton Rd. ST2—3C 24
Gravelly Bank. ST3—1E 34
Grayling Gro. ST6—2K 17
Gray's Clo. ST7—4D 4
Grayshott Rd. ST6—7G 11
Greasley Rd. ST2—7F 19
Greatbatch Av. ST4—7C 22
Greatoak Rd. ST7—1F 15
Greenacres Av. ST11—7H 31
Greenbank Rd. ST5—3K 21
Greenbank Rd. ST6—2H 17
Green Clo. ST11—1J 35
Green Clo. ST12—7G 33
Greendock St. ST3—4A 30
Greendrive. ST7—7D 2
Greenfield. ST8—5B 6
Greenfield Av. ST6—5G 13
Greenfield Clo. ST6—5G 13
Greenfield Pl. ST6—5G 13
Greenfields Rd. ST7—1E 8
Greenfields Rd. ST9—4J 13
Greengate Rd. ST7—6F 3
Greengates St. ST6—1G 17
Greenhead St. ST6—5H 17
Greenhill Rd. ST6—6C 12
Green La. ST11—5B 36
Greenmeadow Gro. ST9—6J 13
Greenmoor Av. ST6—4J 11
Greenock Clo. ST5—7G 21
Green Pk. ST11—7K 35
Green Rd. ST4—4B 28
Greenside. ST5—5H 21
Greenside Av. ST9—2G 19
Greenside Clo. ST7—5C 10
Green's La. ST2—3C 24
Green, The. ST5—4K 27
Green, The. ST6—5F 13
Green, The. ST7—7G 3
Green, The. ST9—1F 19
Green, The. ST11—4J 31
Green, The. ST12—6H 33
Greenway. ST3—4H 29
Greenway. ST7—6B 2
Greenway Av. ST6—3K 17
Greenway Bank. ST2—3G 19
Greenway Bank. ST8—2A 12
Greenway Clo. ST7—3F 3
Greenway Hall Rd. ST2—3H 19
Greenway Hall Rd. ST9—2G 19
Greenway Pl. ST2—6F 19
Greenway Rd. ST8—1C 6

Greenways. ST7—3F 15
Greenway, The. ST4—1B 32
Greenway, The. ST5—3K 21
Greenwood Av. ST4—5B 28
Greenwood Rd. ST11—3B 36
Greeting St. ST6—6J 17
Gregory St. ST3—3A 30
Gregson Clo. ST3—4K 29
Grenadier Clo. ST4—4F 33
Grendon Grn. ST2—4B 24
Gresham St. ST1—1E 22
Gresley Way. ST7—3F 15
Gresty St. ST4—7D 22
Greville St. ST1—1G 23
Greyfriars Rd. ST2—1K 23
Greysan Av. ST7—4H 11
Greystones. ST5—6E 16
(off First Av.)
Greyswood Rd. ST4—4B 28
Grice Rd. ST4—6B 22
Griffin St. ST3—3A 30
Grig Pl. ST7—6C 2
Grindley La. ST3—3F 35
Grindley La. ST11—1K 35
Grindley Pl. ST4—1C 28
Grisdale Clo. ST3—1F 35
Gristhorpe Way. ST2—5C 24
Gritter St. ST6—3F 17
Grosvenor Av. ST4—3C 28
Grosvenor Av. ST7—6D 2
Grosvenor Clo. ST7—6D 2
Grosvenor Clo. ST9—4K 13
Grosvenor Gdns. ST6—6K 21
Grosvenor Pl. ST5—1K 21
Grosvenor Pl. ST6—1F 17
Grosvenor Rd. ST3—6E 30
Grosvenor Rd. ST5—6K 21
Grosvenor St. ST3—4A 30
Grove Av. ST4—3H 29
Grove Av. ST7—7G 3
(Church Lawton)
Grove Av. ST7—3A 10
(Kidsgrove)
Grovebank Rd. ST4—4B 28
Grove Ct. ST7—7E 2
Grove Pk. Av. ST7—7G 3
Grove Pl. ST1—4E 22
Grove Rd. ST4—3G 29
Grove St. ST3—3F 21
Grove St. ST6—7J 17
Grove, The. ST5—1J 27
Grove, The. ST6—3K 17
Grove, The. ST7—7G 3
Grove, The. ST11—2K 35
Guernsey Dri. ST5—3F 27
Guernsey Wlk. ST3—4K 29
(off Longton Hall Rd.)
Guildford St. ST4—6F 23
Gun Battery La. ST8—3E 6
Gunn St. ST8—3A 6
Guy St. ST2—2A 24
Gwenys Cres. ST3—3H 29
Gwyn Av. ST8—6B 6

Hackett Clo. ST3—3C 30
Hackwood Clo. ST12—4J 33
Hadden St. ST9—4G 25
Haddon Gro. ST5—7B 16
Haddon Pl. ST2—1B 24
Hadfield Grn. ST6—3B 18
(off Heath Rd.)
Hadleigh Clo. ST5—5J 27
Hadleigh Rd. ST2—7F 19
Hadrian Way. ST5—1E 20
Haig St. ST3—5C 30
Hailsham Clo. ST6—7H 11
Hales Pl. ST3—6B 30
Halesworth Cres. ST5—5K 27
Halfway Pl. ST5—5F 21
Halifax Clo. ST3—1H 35
Haliford Av. ST1—6B 18
Hallahan Gro. ST4—6D 22
Hallam St. ST4—1G 29
Halldearn Av. ST11—4J 31
Hall Dri. ST3—3A 30
Hall Dri. ST7—1C 8
Hall Pl. ST5—1A 22
Halls Rd. ST7—4E 4

Halls Rd. ST8—2A 6
Hall St. ST5—5J 21
Hall St. ST6—5G 17
Hall St. ST7—3D 14
Halton Grn. ST3—7H 29
Hambleton Pl. ST8—6K 5
Hamble Way. ST2—5C 24
Hambro Pl. ST6—5K 11
Hamil Rd. ST6—5J 17
Hamilton Ct. ST5—5K 21
Hamilton Ind. Cen. ST4—2H 29
Hamilton Rise. ST2—1F 19
Hamilton Rd. ST3—5C 30
Hamilton St. ST4—2F 29
Hamlet Pl. ST6—2C 18
Hammersley St. ST1—7C 18
Hammerton Pl. ST2—4J 23
Hammond Av. ST6—5F 13
Hammond Ho. ST1—4G 23
Hammond Rd. ST5—5A 16
Hammoon Gro. ST2—4A 24
Hamner Grn. ST2—6C 24
Hampshire Clo. ST9—5K 13
Hampstead Gro. ST4—1F 33
Hampton St. ST1—4G 23
Hams Clo. ST8—4A 6
Hanbridge Av. ST5—7C 16
Hanchurch La. ST4—7J 27
Hancock St. ST4—7F 23
Handel Gro. ST1—7E 18
Handley Dri. ST8—2K 11
Handley St. ST7—2J 11
Handsacre Rd. ST3—2C 30
Hand St. ST6—3G 17
Hanley Mall. ST1—2F 23
(off Stafford St.)
Hanley Rd. ST6 & ST2—2A 18
Hanover Ct. ST5—5K 21
(off Hanover St.)
Hanover St. ST1—2F 23
Hanover St. ST5—5K 21
(in two parts)
Harber St. ST3—4B 30
Harcourt Av. ST3—6E 30
Harcourt St. ST1—4E 22
Hardewick Clo. ST9—3G 25
Hardinge St. ST4—1G 29
Harding Rd. ST1—4F 23
Hardings Row. ST7—4F 5
Hardingswood Ind. Est. ST7
—2A 10
Hardingswood Rd. ST7—2A 10
Harding Ter. ST4—1D 28
Hardman St. ST2—4E 18
Hardwick Clo. ST4—4E 32
Hardy St. ST6—1F 17
Harebell Gro. ST7—3H 11
Harecastle Av. ST7—3A 10
Hareshaw Gro. ST6—4J 11
Harewood St. ST6—2F 17
Hargreave Clo. ST3—1H 35
Harington Dri. ST3—2D 30
Harlech Av. ST3—6D 30
Harlech Dri. ST8—5A 6
Harlequin Dri. ST6—3A 18
Harley St. ST1—3G 23
Harold St. ST6—4A 18
Harper Av. ST5—2H 21
Harper St. ST6—6G 17
Harpfield Rd. ST4—1B 28
Harptree Wlk. ST4—5C 28
Harpur Cres. ST7—6B 2
Harriseahead La. ST7—7E 4
Harrison Clo. ST7—7D 14
Harrison Ct. ST5—6K 21
(off Occupation St.)
Harrison Rd. ST6—2C 18
Harrison St. ST5—6K 21
Harris St. ST4—6D 22
Harrogate Dri. ST5—4A 20
Harrop St. ST1—7B 18
Harrowby Dri. ST5—3G 27
Harrowby Rd. ST3—7F 31
Hart Ct. ST5—5J 21
Hartill St. ST4—6F 23
Hartington St. ST5—1J 21
Hartland Av. ST6—3A 18
Hartley St. ST6—3A 18
Hartshill Rd. ST4—5A 22
Hartwell. ST5—3G 27

Hartwell La. ST12 & ST3
—6K 33
Hartwell Rd. ST3—7F 31
Harvey Rd. ST3—5F 31
Haslemere Av. ST2—4F 19
Hassall Rd. CW11 & ST7—3A 2
Hassall St. ST1—3G 23
Hassam Av. ST5—4H 21
Hassall St. ST5—6J 21
Hatfield Cres. ST3—7H 29
Hathersage Clo. ST3—2B 30
Hatherton Clo. ST5—3K 15
Hatrell St. ST5—6K 21
Havelet Dri. ST5—4G 27
Havelock Gro. ST8—4A 6
Havelock Pl. ST11—4E 22
Haven Av. ST6—5B 18
Haven Cres. ST9—2G 25
Haven Gro. ST5—6E 16
Havergal Wlk. ST3—2B 30
Hawes St. ST6—1F 17
Hawkesdale Clo. ST3—1F 35
Hawkins St. ST4—1G 29
Hawkstone Clo. ST5—6K 21
Hawthorne Av. ST4—2B 28
Hawthorne Av. ST7—4F 15
Hawthorn Gdns. ST4—4K 9
Hawthorn Pl. ST3—6E 30
Hawthorn Rd. ST5—4A 16
Hawthorn St. ST6—7J 17
Hawthorn Vs. ST7—1G 9
Haydon St. ST4—4B 22
Hayes St. ST6—3A 18
Hayeswood La. ST7—7D 14
Hayfield Cres. ST4—7H 23
Hayfield Rd. ST5—5C 20
Hayhead Clo. ST4—2D 10
Hayling Pl. ST3—4J 29
Haymarket. ST6—2F 17
Hayner Gro. ST3—3G 31
Haywood Rd. ST6—3J 17
Haywood St. ST4—5E 22
Hazel Clo. ST4—2C 28
Hazel Clo. ST7—1D 10
Hazeldene Rd. ST4—1F 33
Hazel Gro. ST3—5E 30
Hazel Gro. ST7—1G 9
Hazel Gro. ST8—2F 7
Hazelhurst Rd. ST6—6H 11
Hazelhurst St. ST11—4G 23
Hazel Rd. ST5—5K 15
Hazelwood Rd. ST9—6J 13
Hazlitt Way. ST3—2D 30
Heakley Av. ST6—1D 18
Healey Av. ST8—6K 5
Healey Pl. ST3—5B 30
Heanor Pl. ST4—4K 29
Heath Av. ST5—3K 21
Heath Av. ST7—3E 2
Heath Av. ST9—2K 25
Heathcote Ct. ST3—2C 30
Heathcote Rise. ST3—3G 31
Heathcote Rd. ST3—4K 29
Heathcote Rd. ST7—6E 14
Heathcote St. ST3—1A 30
Heathcote St. ST5—5A 16
Heathcote St. ST7—3B 10
Heath Ct. ST7—5F 3
Heathdene Clo. ST3—3A 30
Heath End Rd. ST7—5B 2
Heather Clo. ST9—2G 25
Heather Cres. ST3—4F 35
Heather Hills. ST9—7H 13
Heatherlands Clo. ST3—3E 34
Heatherleigh Gro. ST1—7D 18
Heathfield Ct. ST6—5E 10
Heathfield Dri. ST5—4K 15
Heathfield Gro. ST3—2E 34
Heathfield Rd. ST6—7A 12
Heath Gro. ST3—3F 35
Heath Ho. La. ST2—2J 23
Heath Pl. ST5—3K 21
Heathside La. ST6—7C 12
Heath's Pas. ST3—4C 30
Heath St. ST5—7B 16
(Chesterton)
Heath St. ST5—5J 21
(Newcastle)
Heath St. ST6—5E 10
Heath St. ST8—4A 6

Heathwood Dri. ST7—6B 2
Heaton Ter. ST5—7D 16
Heaton Ter. ST9—3K 13
Heaton Vs. ST6—5G 13
Heber St. ST3—3B 30
Hedley Pl. ST5—5G 21
Helena St. ST4—1H 29
Hellyar-Brook Rd. ST7—7B 2
Helston Av. ST3—4D 30
Heming Pl. ST2—3K 23
Hemingway Rd. ST3—3C 30
Hempstalls Ct. ST5—4J 21
Hempstalls Gro. ST3—3J 21
Hempstalls La. ST5—3K 21
Hemsby Way. ST5—5J 27
Henderson Gro. ST3—4G 31
Henley Av. ST8—5J 5
Henley Clo. ST12—3H 33
Henry St. ST6—1F 17
Henshall Pl. ST6—6F 11
Henshall Rd. ST5—5A 16
Herbert Rd. ST3—5C 30
Herbert St. ST4—1G 29
Herd St. ST6—4H 17
Hereford Av. ST5—3K 27
Hereford Gro. ST2—4C 24
Herm Clo. ST5—3F 27
Hermes Clo. ST3—1H 35
Heron St. ST4—2H 29
Hertford Gro. ST5—3A 28
Hertford St. ST4—3H 29
Hesketh Av. ST6—7B 12
Heskin Way. ST6—6J 11
Hester Clo. ST3—1B 30
Hethersett Wlk. ST2—5C 24
Hewitt Cres. ST9—3G 25
Hewitt St. ST6—6H 11
Heyburn Cres. ST6—5G 17
Heyfield Cotts. ST12—7E 32
Heysham Clo. ST3—3G 31
Hickman St. ST5—5J 21
Hick St. ST5—6J 21
Hide St. ST4—7E 22
High Bank Pl. ST6—4K 17
Highcroft Wlk. ST6—3K 17
Higher Ash Rd. ST7—4K 9
Higherland. ST5—6H 21
Higherland Ct. ST7—2C 10
(off Attwood St.)
Highfield Av. ST3—6E 30
Highfield Av. ST5—2A 22
Highfield Av. ST7—2D 10
Highfield Clo. ST11—1J 35
Highfield Dri. ST3—3H 29
Highfield Grange. ST5—2B 22
Highfield Pl. ST8—3B 6
Highfield Rd. E. ST8—4B 6
Highfield Rd. W. ST8—4B 6
Highgate Clo. ST6—1C 18
Highgrove Rd. ST4—4C 28
Highland Clo. ST8—3F 7
Highland Clo. ST11—1K 35
High La. ST5—1A 20
High La. ST6—7E 12
(Brown Edge)
High La. ST6—6J 11 to 4K 17
(Stoke-on-Trent)
High St. Biddulph, ST8—3A 6
High St. Bignall End, ST7
—4G 15
High St. Caverswall, ST11
—4K 31
High St. Chesterton, ST5
—6A 16
High St. Halmer End, ST7
—6C 14
High St. Harriseahead, ST7
—7G 5
High St. Knutton, ST5—3F 21
High St. May Bank, ST5—3A 22
High St. Mow Cop, ST7—4F 5
High St. Newcastle, ST5—5J 21
High St. Newchapel, ST7
—2G 11
High St. Rookery, ST7—1E 10
High St. Silverdale, ST5—4B 20
High St. Stoke-on-Trent, ST6
—5E 10 to 2F 17
High St. Talke Pits, ST7—6K 9
High St. Wolstanton, ST5
—7E 16

Highton St. ST2—4G 19
High View. ST3—3F 35
High View Rd. ST9—4K 13
Highview Rd. ST11—7K 35
Highville Pl. ST4—2C 28
Highway La. ST5—7A 20
Higson Av. ST4—6D 22
Hilderstone Rd. ST3 & ST15
—4E 34
Hillary Rd. ST7—1D 10
Hillary St. ST6—7K 17
Hillberry Clo. ST2—4K 23
Hillchurch St. ST1—2F 23
Hillcott Wlk. ST3—4C 30
(off Kendrick St.)
Hill Cres. ST7—7F 15
Hillcrest Ho. ST1—2G 23
Hillcrest St. ST1—2G 23
Hillfield Av. ST4—3B 28
Hillgreen Rd. ST3—2C 30
Hillman St. ST2—4F 19
Hillport Av. ST5—6D 16
Hillport Ho. ST5—6E 16
(off Claremont Clo.)
Hillside. ST5—6H 21
Hillside Av. ST3—6E 30
Hillside Av. ST7—5C 10
Hillside Av. ST9—4K 13
Hillside Av. ST11—3B 36
Hillside Clo. ST2—2G 19
Hillside Clo. ST7—4F 5
Hillside Clo. ST8—2F 7
Hillside Clo. ST11—7K 35
Hillside Rd. ST2—2G 19
Hillside Rd. ST9—2G 25
Hillside Wlk. ST4—6A 22
Hill St. ST4—7D 22
Hill St. ST5—4H 21
Hillswood Clo. ST9—5J 13
Hillswood Dri. ST9—4J 13
Hill Ter. ST7—3D 14
Hill Top. ST6—3F 13
Hilltop Av. ST5—4B 22
Hill Top Cres. ST3—3F 35
Hill View. ST2—3F 19
Hilton Rd. ST4—6A 22
Hincho Pl. ST6—1C 18
Hinckley Gro. ST4—3E 32
Hines St. ST4—2H 29
Hinton Clo. ST3—7J 29
Hitchman St. ST4—1H 29
Hobart St. ST6—6J 17
Hobson St. ST6—5J 17
Hodgkinson St. ST5—7B 16
Hodnet Gro. ST1—1E 22
Hogarth Pl. ST5—7A 16
Holbeach Av. ST2—4K 23
Holborn. ST5—6K 21
Holbrook Wlk. ST2—5B 24
Holdcroft Rd. ST2—1B 24
Holden Av. ST5—3A 22
Holden Av. N. ST6—5B 18
Holden Av. S. ST6—5B 18
Holder St. ST11—1E 22
Holding Cres. ST7—7A 16
Holditch Ind. Est. ST5—1G 21
Holditch St. ST5—1G 21
Holecroft St. ST6—5J 17
Holehouse La. ST6 & ST9
—2F 13
Holehouse La. ST7—4J 3
Holehouse Rd. ST7—2F & 7G 19
Holland St. ST6—2F 17
Hollies Dri. ST3—3F 35
Hollies, The. ST5—4K 21
Hollings St. ST4—2K 29
Hollington Dri. ST6—4J 11
Hollins Cres. ST7—3A 10
Hollins Grange. ST7—3K 9
Hollinshead Av. ST5—2J 21
Hollinshead Clo. ST7—4B 4
Hollinwood Clo. ST7—4A 10
Hollinwood Rd. ST7—4A 10
Hollowood Pl. ST6—7C 12
Hollowood Wlk. ST6—7B 12
Hollow, The. ST7—6D 4
Hollow, The. ST11—5K 31
Hollybank Cres. ST4—2D 28
Hollybush Cres. ST3—3H 29
Hollybush Rd. ST3—4H 29
Holly Dri. ST2—3F 25

Holly La. ST7—1E 8
(Alsager)
Holly La. ST7—6G 5
(Harriseahead)
Holly Pl. ST4—3H 29
Holly Rd. ST5—4K 15
Holly Tree Dri. ST8—1A 6
Hollywall La. ST6—1D 16
Hollywood La. ST5—5A 20
Holmesfield Wlk. ST3—4C 30
Holmes Way. ST6—4K 11
Holst Dri. ST1—7E 18
Holyhead Cres. ST3—3G 31
Homer Pl. ST6—7K 11
Homer St. ST1—2H 23
Homestead St. ST2—6C 24
Homestead, The. ST2—2G 19
Homestead, The. ST5—4A 22
Honeysuckle Av. ST11—5A 36
Honeywall. ST4—7D 22
Honeywall Ho. ST4—7D 22
Honeywood. ST5—4J 21
Honiton Wlk. ST3—4C 30
Hoon Av. ST5—2J 21
Hoover St. ST6—2F 17
Hopedale Clo. ST4—7A 24
Hopedale Clo. ST5—4J 27
Hope St. ST1—2F 23
Hope St. ST7—2F 15
Hopton Way. ST6—4J 11
Hopwood Pl. ST2—3A 24
Horatius Rd. ST5—7K 15
Hordley St. ST1—3G 23
Horleston St. ST1—1F 23
Hornby Row. ST4—7D 22
Horsley Gro. ST3—7H 29
Horton Dri. ST3—2F 31
Horton St. ST5—5A 22
Horwood Gdns. ST5—1D 26
Horwood Gdns. ST6—4A 18
(off Cliff St.)
Hose St. ST6—2F 17
Hoskins Rd. ST6—7G 11
Hot La. ST6—6K 17
Hot La. ST8—2F 7
Hot La. Ind. Est. ST6—5K 17
Hougher Wall Rd. ST7—4D 14
Hough Hill. ST6—3F 13
Houghton St. ST1—4F 23
Houghwood La. ST9—1H 19
Houldsworth Dri. ST6—5K 11
Housefield Rd. ST2—6C 24
Houseman Dri. ST3—2D 30
Houston Av. ST9—4J 13
Hoveringham Dri. ST2—5J 23
Howard Clo. ST9—2G 25
Howard Cres. ST1—4H 23
Howard Gro. ST5—1H 27
Howard Pl. ST11—4E 22
Howard Pl. ST5—1H 27
Howard St. ST3—5B 30
Howard Wlk. ST3—5B 30
Howe Gro. ST5—4F 21
Howson St. ST1—3G 23
Hudson Wlk. ST3—3B 30
Hugh Bourne Pl. ST8—2K 11
Hughes Av. ST5—4H 21
Hughes St. ST6—6J 17
Hughson Gro. ST6—2C 18
Hulland St. ST5—5C 20
Hullock's Pool Rd. ST7—7D 8
Hulme Clo. ST5—5C 20
Hulme La. ST3 & ST9—4F 25
Hulme Rd. ST3—2E 30
Hulme St. ST4—6B 22
Hulse St. ST4—1A 30
Hulton Rd. ST2—7F 19
Hulton St. ST1—1G 23
Humber Dri. ST8—3C 6
Humbert St. ST1—3C 22
Humber Way. ST5—3J 27
Hunsford Clo. ST3—3B 30
(off Goddard St.)
Huntbach St. ST1—2F 23
Hunters Clo. ST8—3A 6
Hunters Dri. ST4—1C 28
Hunters Way. ST4—2C 28
Huntilee Rd. ST6—2G 17
Huntingdon Pl. ST1—7D 18
Huntley Av. ST4—1D 28
Hunt St. ST6—2G 17

Stoke 45

Huron Gro. ST4—7D 28
Hurst Clo. ST7—6K 9
Hurst Rd. ST8—1E 6
Hurst St. ST3—4A 30
Hutchinson Wlk. ST3—4K 29
Hutton Way. ST2—4C 24
Huxley Pl. ST3—3C 30
Hyacinth Ct. ST5—4K 21
Hyndley Clo. ST2—3K 23

Ian Rd. ST7—2F 11
Ibsen Rd. ST3—3F 31
Ikins Dri. ST7—3F 15
Ilam Clo. ST5—5C 20
Ilford Side. ST3—7H 29
Ilkley Pl. ST5—4A 20
Imandra Clo. ST4—7D 28
Imogen Clo. ST4—1A 30
Ingelow Clo. ST3—5K 29
Ingestre Sq. ST3—7H 29
Ingleborough Pl. ST2—4H 19
Ingleby Rd. ST3—7H 29
Inglefield Av. ST6—4K 17
Ingleton Gro. ST3—1F 35
Inglewood Dri. ST5—7E 16
Inglewood Gro. ST5—7E 16
Inglis St. ST4—6F 23
Intake Rd. ST6—1B 18
Iona Pl. ST3—4J 29
Ipswich Wlk. ST2—4A 24
Irene Av. ST5—4A 22
Irene Av. ST6—2H 17
Iris Clo. ST3—2H 31
Ironmarket. ST5—5J 21
Irwell St. ST6—7G 17
Isherwood Pl. ST3—3C 30
Islay Wlk. ST3—4K 29
Ivy Clo. ST11—5A 36
Ivy Gro. ST4—7C 28
Ivyhouse Dri. ST12—4H 33
Ivy Ho. Rd. ST1—3H 23
Ivy Ho. Rd. ST8—1A 6
Ivy La. ST7—2E 8

Jack Ashley Ct. ST4—1G 29
Jackfield St. ST6—4K 17
Jack Haye La. ST2—4H 19
Jackson St. ST6—5J 17
Jacqueline St. ST6—1E 16
Jamage Ind. Est. ST7—6J 9
Jamage Rd. ST7—6K 9
James Cres. ST9—2H 25
James St. ST4—2C 28
James St. ST5—1K 21
James Way. ST8—5J 5
Jamieson Clo. ST7—7E 2
Janet Pl. ST1—2H 23
Janson St. ST4—6C 28
Jasmine Clo. ST11—4A 36
Jasmin Way. ST7—2H 11
Jason St. ST5—4H 21
Jasper Clo. ST12—4J 33
Jasper St. ST1—3F 23
Java Cres. ST4—1E 32
Jaycean Av. ST6—1G 17
Jean Clo. ST6—3J 17
Jefferson St. ST6—1F 17
Jenkinson Clo. ST5—6G 21
Jenkins St. ST6—5H 17
Jerbourg Clo. ST5—3F 27
Jeremy Clo. ST4—1C 28
Jersey Clo. ST5—3F 27
Jervison St. ST3—1C 30
Jervis St. ST1—1G 23
Jesmond Gro. ST3—7H 29
Joanhurst Cres. ST1—4E 22
Jodrell View. ST7—4D 10
John Bright St. ST1—1G 23
John O'Gaunt's Rd. ST5—5H 21
Johnson Av. ST5—2H 21
Johnson Pl. ST6—6K 11
Johnson St. ST5—6K 15
Johnstone Av. ST9—2H 25
John St. ST1—3F 23
John St. ST5—5A 16
(Chesterton)
John St. ST5—4F 21
(Knutton)

John St. ST5—5E 16
(Longbridge Hayes)
John St. ST5—5A 22
(Newcastle)
John St. ST7—4K 9
John St. ST8—4A 6
Joiners Sq. Ind. Est. ST1
—4G 23
Jolley St. ST6—4A 18
Jolyon Clo. ST4—1A 30
Jonathan Rd. ST4—4F 33
Jordan St. ST1—4E 22
Joseph Cres. ST7—2F 9
Joseph St. ST6—5G 17
Josiah Wedgwood St. ST1
—3D 22
Joyce Av. ST6—3K 17
Jubilee Av. ST1—3D 22
Jubilee Clo. ST8—4B 6
Jubilee Ct. ST1—3G 23
Jubilee Rd. ST4—7C 28
Jubilee Rd. ST5—3A 22
Judgefield La. ST6—2D 12
Judith Gro. ST4—3F 29
Jug Bank. ST6—7K 17
June Rd. ST4—1A 30
Juniper Clo. ST3—2F 35
Jupiter St. ST6—4A 18
Justin Clo. ST5—7F 17

Kara Pl. ST4—7D 28
Kaydor Clo. ST9—2G 25
Kearsley Way. ST3—7H 29
Keary St. ST4—1E 28
Keats Gdns. ST7—4C 10
Keble Way. ST3—5J 29
Kedleston Rd. ST6—3J 17
Keele Rd. ST5—7A 20 to 6G 21
Keele Science Pk. ST5—7C 20
Keele St. ST6—1F 17
Keele University. ST5—7C 20
Keelings Dri. ST4—3B 28
Keelings Rd. ST1—1G 23
Keelings Ter. ST1—2H 23
(off Keelings Rd.)
Keeling St. ST5—7E 16
Keene Clo. ST6—2C 18
Kelly Grn. ST6—6K 11
Kelman Rd. ST4—1K 29
Kelmore Clo. ST3—3A 30
Kelsall St. ST6—4K 17
Kelsall Way. ST7—4D 14
Kelvin Av. ST1—7B 18
Kelvin St. ST5—2A 22
Kemball Av. ST4—3F 29
Kemnay Av. ST6—4K 11
Kempthorne Rd. ST1—4G 23
Kendal Gro. ST2—4C 24
Kendal Pl. ST5—1J 27
Kendrick St. ST3—4C 30
Kenelyn Cres. ST3—3H 29
Kenilworth Gro. ST3—6E 30
Kenilworth Gro. ST5—3B 22
Kenley Av. ST9—4K 13
Kennedy Rd. ST4—1E 32
Kennedy Wlk. ST9—2G 25
Kennermont Rd. ST2—1B 24
Kennet Clo. ST5—4J 27
Kensington Rd. ST4—3C 28
Kensworth Clo. ST5—4H 27
Kent Dri. ST9—6J 13
Kent Gro. ST5—5K 15
Kentmere Clo. ST4—2A 30
Kentmere Pl. ST5—1J 27
Kent Pl. ST4—1H 29
Kents Row. ST12—6H 33
Kenworthy St. ST6—1G 17
Kersbrook Clo. ST4—2F 33
Kervis Gro. ST3—2G 35
Kesteven Wlk. ST2—3A 24
Kestral Clo. ST8—5K 5
Kestrel Av. ST3—1H 35
Keswick Pl. ST5—1J 27
Kettering Dri. ST2—5J 23
Ketton Clo. ST6—4K 11
Keynsham Wlk. ST6—3B 18
Keyworth Wlk. ST2—4K 23
Kibworth Gro. ST1—1F 23
Kidbrooke Pl. ST3—7G 29
Kidsgrove Bank. ST7—4D 10

Kidsgrove Rd. ST6—4E 10
Kilburn Pl. ST2—4J 23
Kildare St. ST3—5B 30
(in two parts)
Kilndown Clo. ST1—4D 22
Kilsby Gro. ST2—3F 19
Kimberley Grange. ST5—4J 21
Kimberley Rd. ST1—3D 22
Kimberley Rd. ST5—4J 21
Kimberley St. ST3—5A 30
Kinder Pl. ST5—5C 20
Kingcross St. ST3—4B 30
King Edward St. ST3—3A 30
Kingfisher Cres. ST11—7K 35
Kingfisher Gro. ST6—2A 18
King George St. ST1—1G 23
King's Av. ST5—1K 21
Kingsbridge Av. ST5—2J 27
Kingsbury Gro. ST1—7D 18
Kingsclere Gro. ST1—6C 18
King's Croft. ST4—5A 22
Kingsdale Clo. ST3—1F 35
Kingsfield Clo. ST8—3B 6
Kingsfield Oval. ST4—5A 22
Kingsfield Rd. ST4—5A 22
Kingsfield Rd. ST8—3A 6
Kingsford Pl. ST3—7F 31
Kingside Gro. ST4—3F 33
Kingsland Av. ST4—3C 28
Kingsley Clo. ST7—6K 9
Kingsley Rd. ST7—6K 9
Kingsley St. ST3—6F 31
Kingsmead Rd. ST3—1E 34
Kingsnorth Pl. ST3—2G 35
Kings Pl. ST4—4A 22
Kings Rd. ST4—6D 28
Kings Ter. ST4—5A 22
Kingston Av. ST1—6C 18
Kingston Clo. ST2—6C 18
Kingston Pl. ST3—1C 6
King St. ST4 & ST3
—1H 29 to 3A 30
King St. ST5—6A 16
(Chesterton)
King St. ST5—3H 21
(Cross Heath)
King St. ST5—5K 21
(Newcastle)
King St. ST7—4D 14
(Audley)
King St. ST7—2C 10
(Kidsgrove)
King St. ST7—7K 9
(Talke Pits)
King St. ST8—3A 6
Kingsway. ST4—7E 22
Kingsway E. ST5—1J 27
Kingsway W. ST5—1H 27
Kingswell Rd. ST4—5A 22
Kingswinford Pl. ST6—6B 18
Kingswood. ST7—3D 10
King William St. ST6—2G 17
Kinnersley Av. ST7—4B 10
Kinnersley St. ST7—2C 10
Kinsey St. ST5—4C 20
Kinver St. ST6—4A 18
Kipling Way. ST2—5C 24
Kirby St. ST6—7J 17
Kirkbride Clo. ST3—3C 30
Kirkham St. ST4—1D 28
Kirkland La. ST4—7D 22
Kirkstall Pl. ST5—2J 27
Kirk St. ST6—3A 18
Kirkup Wlk. ST3—4A 30
Kirkwall Gro. ST2—3F 19
Knarsdale Clo. ST3—2C 30
Knightsbridge Way. ST6
(off Ladywell Rd.) —2F 17
Knights Croft. ST5—7A 20
Knight St. ST6—1F 17
Knowle Bank Rd. ST7—5A 14
Knowle Rd. ST8—4A 6
Knowle St. ST4—6D 22
Knowsley La. ST7—7A 4
Knutsford Old Rd. ST7—6F 3
Knutsford Rd. ST7—6F 3
Knutton La. ST5—4G 21
Knutton Rd. ST5—1K 21
Knype Clo. ST6—6C 16
Knypersley Rd. ST6—7C 12
Knype Way. ST5—6C 16

Knype Way. ST8—5K 5
Kyffin Rd. ST2—7F 19

Laburnum Clo. ST7—4A 10
Laburnum Clo. ST11—5B 36
Laburnum Gro. ST3—4H 29
Laburnum Pl. ST3—7E 30
Laburnum Pl. ST5—4K 15
Lad La. ST5—5J 21
Ladybank Gro. ST3—7H 29
Ladymoor La. ST6—1F 13
Ladysmith Rd. ST1—3D 22
Ladysmith St. ST3—5A 30
Ladywell Rd. ST6—2F 17
(in two parts)
Lagonda Clo. ST8—6K 5
Lakebrook Clo. ST4—5E 10
Lakewood Dri. ST12—4H 33
Lakewood Gro. ST1—2D 22
Lally Pl. ST8—2K 11
Lambert St. ST6—2G 17
Lambourne Dri. ST2—4G 19
Lambourn Pl. ST3—7G 29
Lamb St. ST1—2F 23
Lamb St. ST7—2C 10
Lamerton Gro. ST3—5E 30
Lamotte Clo. ST4—2A 30
Lanark Wlks. ST5—7G 21
Lancaster Av. ST5—6A 22
Lancaster Cres. ST4—6A 22
Lancaster Dri. ST6—1D 18
Lancaster Rd. ST5—6A 22
Lancester Av. ST11—7K 35
Lanchester Clo. ST5—5K 5
Lancia Clo. ST8—6K 5
Lander Pl. ST6—6A 12
Landon St. ST3—4B 30
Landrake Gro. ST6—5K 11
Landseer Pl. ST5—7A 16
Lane Farm Gro. ST1—6C 18
Lanehead Rd. ST1—3C 22
Langdale Cres. ST1—6B 18
Langdale Rd. ST5—2J 27
Langford Rd. ST2—3A 24
Langford Rd. ST5—3H 21
Langham Rd. ST2—4E 18
Langland Dri. ST3—5J 29
Langley St. ST4—5A 22
Langton St. ST9—2F 25
Lansbury Gro. ST3—4G 31
Lansdell Av. ST5—7C 16
Lansdowne Cres. ST9—2G 25
Lansdowne Rd. ST4—6B 22
Lansdowne St. ST3—6A 30
Larch Clo. ST7—4C 10
Larch Gro. ST3—5H 29
Larchmount Clo. ST4—1E 32
Larch Pl. ST5—5A 16
Larch Wood. ST5—1B 26
Larkfield. ST7—3D 10
Larkin Av. ST3—3C 30
Larksfield Rd. ST6—4B 18
Larkspur Gro. ST5—4K 21
Lascelles St. ST6—2F 17
Lask Edge Rd. ST8 & ST13
—3G 7
Laski Cres. ST3—5G 31
Latebrook Clo. ST6—5E 10
Latham Gro. ST6—5K 11
Latimer Way. ST2—4B 24
Lauder Pl. N. ST2—7D 24
Lauder Pl. S. ST2—7D 24
Laundry Ho. ST4—1B 32
Laurel Cres. ST9—3F 25
Laurel Dri. ST7—1G 11
Laurel St. ST3—5G 29
Lauren Clo. ST4—1H 29
Lavender Av. ST11—5A 36
Lavender Clo. ST3—2H 31
Lawley St. ST3—4C 30
Lawrence St. ST1—4E 22
Lawson Ter. ST5—7D 16
Lawton Av. ST7—1K 9
Lawton Coppice. ST7—7A 4
Lawton Cres. ST8—3B 6
Lawtongate Est. ST7—6G 3
Lawton Heath Rd. ST7—5F 3
Lawton Rd. ST7—7D 2
Lawton St. ST6—3J 17
Lawton St. ST7—7E 4
Lawton St. ST8—3B 6

Laxey Rd. ST5—4H 21
Laxton Gro. ST4—4F 33
Leacroft Rd. ST3—7F 31
Leadbeater Av. ST4—2C 28
Leadendale La. ST3—5D 34
Leaford Wlk. ST2—4J 23
Leaks All. ST3—5A 30
Leamington Gdns. ST5—3B 22
Lea Pl. ST3—5G 31
Leaside Rd. ST4—2B 28
Leason Rd. ST3—5F 31
Leason St. ST4—7E 22
Leaswood Clo. ST5—5K 27
Leaswood Pl. ST5—5K 27
Lea, The. ST4—1E 32
Lea Way. ST7—1D 8
Leawood Rd. ST4—4B 28
Ledbury Cres. ST1—1J 23
Ledstone Way. ST3—3D 30
Leech Av. ST5—7B 16
Leech St. ST5—6K 21
(in two parts)
Leeds St. ST4—2J 29
Lee Gro. ST5—3J 27
Leek La. ST8—3F 7
Leek New Rd. ST2, ST6 & ST9
—7K 17 to 1H 19
Leek Rd. ST3 & ST9
—1G 31 to 3K 25
Leek Rd. ST4, ST1 & ST2
—6F 23 to 4F 19
Leek Rd. ST6—5G 13
Leek Rd. ST9—7H 13
Leese St. ST4—7E 22
Legge St. ST5—6K 21
Leicester Av. ST7—6C 2
Leicester Clo. ST5—2K 27
Leicester Pl. ST2—4B 24
Leigh La. ST6—4E 16
Leigh St. ST6—3J 17
Leighton Clo. ST9—1G 19
Lennox Rd. ST3—5C 30
Leonard Av. ST2—2F 19
Leonard Dri. ST5—5F 13
Leonard St. ST6—3K 17
Leonora St. ST6—6H 17
Leopold St. ST4—1H 29
Lessways Clo. ST5—5C 16
Lessways Wlk. ST6—6H 17
Lester Clo. ST7—7D 2
Leveson Rd. ST4—6C 28
Leveson St. ST3—5B 30
Levita Rd. ST4—3C 28
Lewisham Dri. ST6—5E 10
Lewis St. ST4—6E 22
Lexham Pl. ST3—5D 30
Leyfield Rd. ST4—2E 32
Ley Gdns. ST3—4K 29
Leyland Grn. ST6—5J 11
(off Coppull Pl.)
Leys Dri. ST5—3F 27
Leys La. ST2—3G 19
Libra Pl. ST6—6H 11
Lichfield Clo. ST5—4D 20
Lichfield Rd. ST7—5K 9
Lichfield St. ST1—3F 23
Liddle St. ST4—1D 28
Lidgate Wlk. ST5—5K 27
Lightwater Gro. ST2—4D 18
Lightwood Rd. ST3
—5B 30 to 4D 34
Lilac Clo. ST3—2H 31
Lilac Clo. ST5—4K 15
Lilac Gro. ST3—4H 29
Lilleshall Rd. ST5—2A 28
Lilleshall St. ST3—5B 30
Lillydale Rd. ST2—3A 24
Lily St. ST5—1K 21
Limbrick Rd. ST7—4A 14
Lime Clo. ST3—2H 31
Lime Gro. ST7—2E 8
Lime Gro. ST12—4J 33
Lime Heath Pl. ST6—7G 11
Lime Kiln La. ST7—2A 10
Limes, The. ST5—6E 16
Lime St. ST4—2E 28
Limewood Clo. ST11—5B 36
Linacre Way. ST3—2D 30
Lincoln Av. ST5—2K 27
Lincoln Gro. ST5—2K 27

Lincoln Rd. ST6—6J 17
Lincoln Rd. ST7—2B 10
Lincoln St. ST1—3G 23
Lindale Gro. ST3—1G 35
Linda Rd. ST6—7G 11
Linden Clo. ST5—3J 21
Linden Dri. ST8—2A 6
Linden Gro. ST5—3J 21
Linden Pl. ST3—6J 29
Lindley Pl. ST3—4F 35
Lindley St. ST6—6K 17
Lindop St. ST1—2G 23
(off Linfield Rd.)
Lindop St. ST1—2G 23
Lindsay St. ST1—3E 22
Lindsay Way. ST7—7A 2
Lindum St. ST4—1F 33
Linfield Rd. ST1—2G 23
Lingard St. ST6—5J 17
Lingfield Av. ST6—4E 12
Linhope Gro. ST3—1G 35
Linkend Clo. ST1—1J 23
Links Av. ST5—2J 21
Linley Gro. ST7—1F 9
Linley La. ST7—7F 3
Linley Rd. ST4—6A 22
Linley Rd. ST7—1F 9
(Alsager)
Linley Rd. ST7—3H 9
(Talke)
Linley Trading Est. ST7—3J 9
Linnburn Rd. ST3—3C 30
Linwood Way. ST6—7G 11
Lionel Gro. ST4—7B 22
Lion Gro. ST5—5A 16
Lion St. ST4—7D 22
Lisbon Pl. ST5—7F 21
Liskeard Clo. ST2—5K 23
Lit. Bleedingwolf La. ST7
—6A 4
Lit. Chell La. ST6—7H 11
Lit. Cliffe Rd. ST3—3H 29
Lit. Eaves La. ST7—7G 19
Little-field. ST4—3B 28
Little La. ST3—4D 34
Lit. Moss Clo. ST7—6A 4
Lit. Moss La. ST7—6A 4
Liverpool Rd. ST4—7E 22
Liverpool Rd. ST5—1H & 5J 21
(Newcastle, in two parts)
Liverpool Rd. ST5—2K 15
(Red Street)
Liverpool Rd. ST7—2B 10
Liverpool Rd. E. ST7—1K 9
Liverpool Rd. W. ST7—7F 3
Livingstone St. ST6—3A 18
Lloyd St. ST3—5B 30
Locketts La. ST3—5B 30
Lockett St. ST1—7B 18
Lockington Av. ST2—4C 24
Lockley St. ST1—1H 23
Lockwood St. ST2—2F 19
Lockwood St. ST5—5A 22
Lodge Barn Rd. ST8—5D 6
Lodge Gro. ST5—7E 16
Lodge Rd. ST4—7B 22
Lodge Rd. ST7—7C 2
(Alsager)
Lodge Rd. ST7—6K 9
(Talke Pits)
Loftus St. ST1—1E 22
Loganbeck Gro. ST3—2D 30
Lomas St. ST4—4D 22
Lombardy Gro. ST3—5F 31
Lomond Wlk. ST3—1J 33
London Rd. ST4—4B 28
London Rd. ST5—5A 16
(Chesterton)
London Rd. ST5—6K 21
(Newcastle)
Longbridge Hayes Rd. ST5
—5E 16
Longbrook Av. ST3—5J 29
Longclough Rd. ST5—3K 15
Longdoles Av. ST3—4D 30
Longfield Rd. ST4—6A 22
Longford Wlk. ST2—4K 23
Long La. ST7—7G 5
Longley Rd. ST3—2B 30
Long Meadow. ST5—4K 27
Longnor Pl. ST2—4K 23

Longport Rd. ST6—6F 17
Long Row. ST7—3C 10
Long Row. ST11—4J 31
Longsdon Gro. ST3—3D 30
Longshaw Av. ST5—6D 16
Longshaw St. ST6—5F 17
Longton Hall Rd. ST3—5J 29
Longton Rd. ST4—2D 32
Longton Rd. ST12—7H 33
Longton Rd. ST15—7C 34
Long Valley Rd. ST8—1A 6
Longview Av. ST7—7E 2
Longview Clo. ST3—2C 30
Lonsdale St. ST4—1E 28
Lonsdene Clo. ST5—4J 15
Loomer Rd. ST5—1E 20
Loomer Rd. Ind. Est. ST5
—1F 21
Lord Nelson Ind. Est. ST1
(off Commercial Rd.) —3G 23
Lordship La. ST4—7F 23
Lordshire Pl. ST7—2H 11
Lord St. ST6—4A 18
Lord St. ST8—4B 6
Loring Rd. ST5—7D 16
Loring Ter. S. ST5—7E 16
Lorne St. ST6—4J 17
Lorraine St. ST7—3H 11
Lotus Av. ST8—5K 5
Loughborough Wlk. ST3
—3B 30
Louise Dri. ST3—4J 29
Louise St. ST6—4J 17
Louvain Av. ST1—6B 18
Lovage Gro. ST2—3K 23
Lovatt Av. ST5—2H 21
Lovatt St. ST4—6E 22
Love La. CW11—1B 2
Loveston Gro. ST3—3C 30
Lowell Dri. ST3—3D 30
Lwr. Ash Rd. ST7—4A 10
Lwr. Bedford St. ST4—4D 22
Lwr. Bethesda St. ST1—3F 23
Lwr. Bryan St. ST1—1F 23
Lower Cres. ST4—6B 22
Lwr. Foundry St. ST1—2F 23
Lwr. Hadderidge. ST6—5H 17
Lwr. High St. ST7—4F 5
Lowerhurst Dri. ST6—5H 11
Lwr. Mayer St. ST1—1G 23
Lwr. Milehouse La. ST5—4G 21
Lwr. Oxford Rd. ST5—4B 22
Lwr. Spring Rd. ST3—5C 30
Lower St. ST5—5J 21
Lower St. ST6—6J 17
Lowe's Pas. ST3—5C 30
Lowe St. ST4—7E 22
Lowhurst Dri. ST6—5H 11
Lowlands Rd. ST6—1C 16
Lowndes Clo. ST4—1C 28
Low St. ST7—3E 2
(in two parts)
Lowther St. ST1—1E 22
Lowthorpe Way. ST2—5D 24
Loxley Pl. ST3—1E 34
Lucas St. ST6—5G 17
Lucerne Pl. ST5—7F 21
Ludbrook Rd. ST4—2A 30
Ludford Clo. ST5—3K 15
Ludlow St. ST1—2G 23
Ludwall Rd. ST3—6D 30
Lugano Clo. ST5—1G 27
Lukesland Av. ST4—1B 28
Luke St. ST6—6G 17
Lulworth Gro. ST6—6H 11
Lundy Rd. ST3—4J 29
Lydford Pl. ST4—8E 30
Lydia Dri. ST1—7D 18
Lyme Brook Pl. ST4—4B 28
Lyme Ct. ST5—7K 21
(off Leech St.)
Lyme Gro. ST5—3K 21
Lyme Rd. ST3—6G 31
Lymes Rd. ST5—1A 26
Lymevale Rd. ST4—3B 28
Lyme Valley Rd. ST5—6J 21
Lymewood Clo. ST5—6J 21
Lymewood Gro. ST5—7J 22
Lyminster Gro. ST2—4F 19
Lynam St. ST4—7D 22
Lyndhurst Dri. ST8—5J 5

Lyndhurst St. ST6—5G 17
Lyneside Rd. ST8—5K 5
Lynmouth Clo. ST8—5K 5
Lynmouth Gro. ST6—5H 11
Lynn Av. ST7—4J 9
Lynn St. ST3—2G 31
Lynsey Clo. ST7—6E 14
Lynton Pl. ST7—7D 2
Lynton Rd. ST5—2G 27
Lysander Rd. ST3—1F 35
Lytton St. ST4—7F 23

Macclesfield St. ST6—4K 17
Macdonald Cres. ST3—4F 31
Mace St. ST4—3C 28
McGough St. ST6—2F 17
Machin Cres. ST5—6C 16
Machin St. ST6—1G 17
Macintyre St. ST6—6J 17
McKellin Clo. ST7—3E 14
McKinley St. ST6—1F 17
Maclagan St. ST4—1E 28
Maddock St. ST6—6G 17
Maddock St. ST7—4D 14
Madeira Pl. ST6—2F 17
Madeley St. ST5—5C 20
Madeley St. ST6—1F 17
Madeley Rd. N. ST5—4C 20
Madison St. ST6—1F 17
Mafeking St. ST3—5A 30
Magdalen Rd. ST3—7H 29
Magdalen Wlk. ST3—1H 33
Magnolia Dri. ST6—3D 18
Magnus St. ST6—6H 17
Maidstone Gro. ST2—4B 24
Main St. ST3—2G 31
Malam St. ST1—1F 23
Malcolm Clo. ST2—3F 19
Malcolm Dri. ST2—1B 24
Malham Rd. ST5—3F 21
Mallard Way. ST6—2A 18
Mallorie Rd. ST6—1B 18
Mallowdale Clo. ST4—2F 22
Malpas Wlk. ST6—5E 10
Malstone Av. ST2—3G 19
Malthouse La. ST3—6G 25
Malthouse La. ST12—6H 33
Malthouse Rd. ST2—3A 24
Malt La. ST3—5C 30
Malton Gro. ST6—7F 11
Malvern Av. ST5—4A 20
Malvern Clo. ST4—1D 32
Mandela Way. ST3—5C 30
Mandeville Clo. ST6—2A 18
Manifold Clo. ST5—5C 20
Manifold Rd. ST11—3A 36
Manifold Wlk. ST2—5K 23
Mannin Clo. ST3—3F 31
Mann St. ST3—4H 31
Manor Ct. St. ST4—1C 28
Manor Rd. ST7—4F 5
Manor St. ST4—1H 29
Manse Clo. ST3—3B 30
Mansfield Clo. ST5—5K 27
Mansfield Dri. ST8—6J 5
Maple Av. ST5—4A 16
Maple Av. ST7—2E 8
(Alsager)
Maple Av. ST7—4K 9
(Talke)
Maple Clo. ST6—7E 12
Maple Cres. ST11—5B 36
Maplehurst Clo. ST6—5K 17
Maple Pl. ST3—5G 31
Maple Pl. ST7—4F 3
Marcel Clo. ST4—5D 28
March Rd. ST3—3A 30
Marchwood Ct. ST4—1B 28
Marcus Ind. Est. ST1—3J 23
Margaret Av. ST7—7C 28
Margaret St. ST1—2H 23
Margery Av. ST7—4A 4
Margill Clo. ST1—3E 22
Marina Dri. ST5—3K 21
Marina Rd. ST4—4C 28
Marina Way. ST1—2C 22
Market Arc. ST5—6J 21
Market La. ST1—2F 23
Market La. ST5—6J 21
Market Pas. ST6—5H 17

Market Pl. ST6—5H 17
Market Sq. ST1—2F 23
(in two parts)
Market St. ST3—3B 30
Market St. ST7—3C 10
Marlborough Clo. ST9—4J 13
Marlborough Rd. ST3—3B 30
Marlborough St. ST4—2G 29
Marldon Pl. ST6—6E 10
Marlow Clo. ST3—2C 30
Marlow Rd. ST3—2C 30
Marney Wlk. ST6—3K 17
Marriott St. ST4—2K 29
Marsden St. ST1—2G 23
Marshall Av. ST6—5F 13
Marshall St. ST6—4H 17
Marsh Av. ST5—1K 21
Marsh Av. ST6—3K 17
Marsh Av. ST7—2G 11
Marsh Clo. ST7—1A 8
Marsh Clo. ST9—2F 25
Marshfield La. ST8—1A 6
Marsh Grn. Clo. ST8—1B 6
Marshgreen Rd. ST8—1B 6
Marsh Gro. ST8—1A 6
Marshland Gro. ST6—4J 11
Marsh La. ST7—1A 8
Marsh Pde. ST5—6K 21
Marsh St. N. ST1—2F 23
Marsh St. S. ST1—2F 23
Marsh View. ST3—3F 35
Marsh Way. ST5—1K 21
Mars St. ST6—4A 18
Marston Gro. ST1—5B 18
Martindale Clo. ST3—7E 30
Martin St. ST6—6A 18
Marychurch Rd. ST2—3A 24
Maryfield Wlk. ST4—1B 28
Maryhill Clo. ST7—1C 10
Maryrose Clo. ST2—3A 24
Masefield Rd. ST3—5K 29
Mason Dri. ST3—3K 5
Mason St. ST4—2J 29
Masterson St. ST4—1G 29
Mathews Ct. ST1—3G 23
(off Wellington St.)
Matlock Pl. ST5—4B 20
Matlock St. ST1—4F 23
Matthews Wlk. ST1—2G 23
(off Bucknall New Rd.)
Maud St. ST4—7H 23
Maunders Rd. ST2—4D 18
Maureen Av. ST6—6F 11
Maureen Gro. ST5—3K 21
Mawdesley St. ST6—7K 17
Mawson Gro. ST4—5G 23
Maxton Way. ST3—5G 31
Maxwell Pl. ST4—7B 22
May Av. ST5—3A 22
May Av. ST6—2G 17
Maybury Way. ST2—3E 18
Mayer Av. ST5—4J 21
Mayer Bank. ST6—5J 17
Mayer St. ST1—2G 23
Mayfair Gdns. ST6—2F 17
(off Wesley St.)
Mayfair Gro. ST9—4J 13
Mayfield St. ST1—1H 23
Mayfield Av. ST5—6H 21
Mayfield Cres. ST1—1H 23
Mayfield Dri. ST11—7J 31
Mayfield Pl. ST5—2K 21
Mayfield Pl. E. ST4—2B 28
Mayfield Pl. W. ST4—2B 28
Mayfield Rd. ST8—5B 6
Maylea Cres. ST6—6A 18
Mayneford St. ST4—6C 28
Mayne St. ST4—5C 28
May Pl. ST4—2A 30
May Pl. ST5—3A 22
May St. ST5—5D 20
May St. ST6—4K 17
Maythorne Rd. ST3—6J 29
Mead Av. ST7—4A 4
Meadow Av. ST3—7B 30
Meadow Av. ST5—2H 21
Meadow Clo. ST11—2K 35
(Blythe Bridge)
Meadow Clo. ST11—3C 36
(Forsbrook)
Meadow Ct. ST12—6F 33

Meadow Croft. ST7—2E 8
Meadowcroft Av. ST3—7H 31
Meadow Dri. ST3—7K 29
Meadow La. ST4—1F 33
Meadow La. ST5—3H 21
Meadow La. ST11—7K 35
Meadow Pl. ST3—6G 31
Meadow Rd. ST6—6F 13
(Brown Edge)
Meadow Rd. ST6—7A 12
(Chell Heath)
Meadow Rd. ST12—6G 33
Meadowside. ST4—1E 32
Meadow Side ST8—5K 5
Meadowside Av. ST7—4C 14
Meadowside La. ST7—4D 4
Meadows Rd. ST7—3B 10
Meadows, The. ST2—5A 24
Meadows, The. ST7—3B 10
Meadows, The. ST9—5K 13
Meadow Stile Caravan Site.
                        ST8—5J 5
Meadow St. ST2—4F 19
Meadow St. ST5—7B 16
Meadow Way. ST7—6G 3
Meads Rd. ST7—7D 2
Mead, The. ST4—1E 32
Meaford Dri. ST3—5H 29
Meaford Rd. ST12—7G 33
Meakin Av. ST5—4J 27
Meakins Row. ST4—2J 29
Medina Way. ST7—2D 10
Medway Dri. ST8—2B 6
Medway Pl. ST5—3J 27
Medway Wlk. ST6—1J 17
Meerbrook Clo. ST4—3E 32
Meere Clo. ST6—2C 18
Megacre. ST7—3G 15
Meigh Rd. ST2 & ST9—3F 25
Meigh St. ST1—2F 23
Meiklejohn Pl. ST6—6J 11
Meirhay Rd. ST3—4C 30
Meir Rd. ST3—6D 30
Meir St. ST6—1G 17
Meir View. ST3—5F 31
Melbourne St. ST3—2C 30
Melfont St. ST6—2G 17
Meliden Way. ST4—1C 28
Mellard St. ST5—4H 21
Mellard St. ST7—4D 14
Mellors Bank. ST7—5F 5
Mellor St. ST7—3H 11
Melrose Av. ST1—6B 18
Melrose Av. ST3—4F 35
Melrose Av. ST5—2H 27
Melstone Av. ST6—2H 17
Melville Ct. ST5—6K 17
Melville Rd. ST3—5D 30
Melville St. ST1—3J 23
Melvyn Cres. ST5—6E 16
Menai Dri. ST8—5B 6
Mendip Grn. ST2—4E 18
Mendip Pl. ST5—3F 21
Menzies Ho. ST3—7E 30
Mercer St. ST3—6A 30
Mercia Cres. ST6—7J 17
Mercury Pl. ST6—4A 18
Mere Ct. ST7—7D 2
Merelake Rd. ST7—3E 8
Meremore Dri. ST5—3K 15
Merevale Av. ST2—4K 23
Meriden Rd. ST5—5K 27
Merlin Clo. ST6—4J 11
Merrial St. ST5—5J 21
Merrick St. ST1—1G 23
Merrion Dri. ST6—3K 17
Mersey Rd. ST5—4H 27
Mersey St. ST1—3E 22
Merton St. ST3—3B 30
Metcalfe Rd. ST6—2J 17
Mews Clo. ST4—2K 23
Mews, The. ST5—2A 22
Michael Clo. ST3—4G 31
Michaels Clo. ST5—6E 16
Michigan Gro. ST4—7E 28
Mickleby Way. ST3—1H 35
Middle Cross St. ST3—3B 30
Middlefield Rd. ST2—6C 24
Middleton Clo. ST6—2C 18
Midfield Clo. ST8—1A 6
Midhurst Clo. ST7—4H 11

Midway Dri. ST11—2K 35
Midway, The. ST5—6J 21
Milan Dri. ST5—1F 27
Milborne Dri. ST5—2K 27
Milburn Rd. ST6—6K 17
Milehouse La. ST5—2J 21
Miles Bank. ST2—2F 23
(off Stafford St.)
Miles Grn. Rd. ST7—5E 14
Milford Av. ST9—2G 25
Milford Rd. ST5—7H 21
Milford St. ST4—2J 29
Milgreen Av. ST1—6B 18
Millbank Pl. ST5—5G 21
Millbank St. ST3—4B 30
Millbridge Clo. ST3—2G 35
Millbrook Gro. ST2—4E 18
Mill Clo. ST11—4H 31
Millend La. ST7—7C 8
Millers La. ST2—4E 18
Millers View. ST7—3C 10
Millett Rd. ST2—3K 23
Millfield Cres. ST2—4E 18
Mill Hayes Rd. ST6—4G 17
Mill Hayes Rd. ST8
                     —1A 12 to 6B 6
Mill Hill Cres. ST6—1J 17
Millicent St. ST4—1H 29
Mill La. ST7—4C 4
Millmead. ST7—4F 3
Mill Rise. ST7—3C 10
Millrise Rd. ST2—4E 18
Millstone Av. ST7—3A 10
Mill St. ST5—5D 20
Millward Rd. ST2—3B 24
Milnes Clo. ST3—5K 29
Milton Cres. ST7—4J 9
Milton Rd. ST1—6B 18
Milton St. ST1—3E 22
Milvale St. ST6—6G 17
Milverton Pl. ST3—3K 29
Milward Gro. ST3—2E 34
Minard Gro. ST3—3F 31
Minden Gro. ST6—5B 18
Minerva Clo. ST8—6K 5
Minerva Rd. ST4—1J 29
Minfield Clo. ST7—4C 10
Minshall St. ST4—2F 29
Minster St. ST6—4K 17
Minton Pl. ST5—1A 22
Minton St. ST4—6B 22
Minton St. ST5—1A 22
Miranda Gro. ST6—4B 18
Mistley Wlk. ST6—5E 10
Mitchell Av. ST7—3K 9
Mitchell Dri. ST7—3K 9
Mitchell St. ST6—4H 17
Moat La. ST7—3A 14
Moat, The. ST3—3G 31
Mobberley Rd. ST6—4E 10
Moffat Gro. ST2—7D 24
Moffatt Way. ST5—4A 20
Mollison Rd. ST3—7F 31
Monaco St. ST5—7F 21
Monkleigh Clo. ST4—3E 32
Monks Clo. ST5—1K 27
Monkton Clo. ST3—6K 29
Monmouth Pl. ST5—3A 28
Monsal Gro. ST1—1J 23
Montfort Pl. ST5—1J 27
Montgomery Pl. ST3—5G 31
Montrose St. ST4—2J 29
Monty Pl. ST4—2A 30
Monument Clo. ST12—6D 32
Monument La. ST12—6D 32
Monument Rd. ST7—6K 9
Monument View. ST7—3F 15
Monyash Clo. ST3—1H 35
Moor Clo. ST8—2C 6
Moorcroft Av. ST5—4J 27
Moore St. ST6—6J 17
Moorfield Av. ST8—3A 6
Moorhead Dri. ST9—1K 19
Moorhouse Av. ST7—7D 2
Moorland Av. ST9—2G 25
Moorland Clo. ST9—2G 25
Moorland Rd. ST6—5H 17
Moorland Rd. ST7—4F 5
Moorland Rd. ST8—3B 6
Moorland View. ST6—2A 18

Moorside Rd. ST9—2J 25
Moorson Av. ST3—3B 4
Moorsyde Rd. ST4—2B 28
Moorthorne Cres. ST5—7C 16
Moran Gro. ST6—6G 17
Moran St. ST5—4G 21
Moresby Clo. ST2—4F 19
Moreton Av. ST5—7A 28
Moreton Clo. ST7—4D 10
Moreton Clo. ST9—4G 13
Moreton Dri. ST7—1C 8
Moreton Ho. ST5—2A 22
Moreton Pde. ST5—2A 22
Morgan Way. ST6—6J 11
Morley St. ST1—3E 22
Mornington Rd. ST1—5B 18
Morpeth St. ST3—4B 30
Morris Sq. ST5—1A 22
Morston Dri. ST5—5J 27
Mortimer Pl. ST3—3E 30
Morton St. ST6—6G 17
Morville Clo. ST7—4H 23
Mosedale Av. ST3—7E 30
Moss Clo. ST9—2G 25
Mossfield Rd. ST3—1C 30
Moss Fields. ST7—1A 8
Moss Hill. ST9—7H 13
Mossland Rd. ST3—2B 30
Moss La. ST7—7A 4
Moss Pk. Av. ST9—2F 25
Moss Pl. ST7—1D 10
Moss Rise. ST5—6K 27
Moss Side. ST7—5C 18
Moss St. ST6—7C 12
Moss Way. ST7—1A 8
Moston St. ST1—1G 23
Mott Pl. ST6—5G 17
Moulton Rd. ST3—3A 30
Mount Av. ST4—7C 22
Mount Clo. ST9—2H 25
Mountfield Pl. ST4—1G 29
Mountford St. ST6—4H 17
Mount Pl. ST11—4B 36
Mt. Pleasant. ST1—3E 22
Mt. Pleasant. ST5—7A 16
(Chesterton)
Mt. Pleasant. ST5—6K 21
(Newcastle)
Mt. Pleasant. ST7—4D 4
Mt. Pleasant Rd. ST7—4D 4
Mount Rd. ST7—3C 10
Mount Rd. ST11—4B 36
Mountsorrel Clo. ST4—2F 33
Mount St. ST1—1G 23
Mount St. ST5—7A 16
Mount, The. ST5—7A 16
Mount, The. ST7—3C 10
(Kidsgrove)
Mount, The. ST7—4A 4
(Scholar Green)
Mousley St. ST6—5G 17
Mowbray Wlk. ST1—5D 18
Mow Cop Rd. ST7—5E 4
Mow La. ST7 & ST8
                     —1J 5 to 1B 6
(Gillow Heath, Biddulph)
Mow La. ST7—6C 4
(Mow Cop)
Moxley Av. ST1—6B 18
Mulberry Pl. ST5—5A 16
Mulberry St. ST1—3G 23
Mulgrave St. ST1—1E 22
Mulliner Clo. ST2—3C 24
Munro St. ST4—2D 28
Munster Ter. ST4—2C 28
Murdock St. ST3—3A 30
Murhall St. ST6—5G 17
Murray St. ST6—5E 10
Myatt St. ST1—2G 23
Mynors St. ST1—2G 23
Myott Av. ST5—7H 21
Myrtle Av. ST3—4G 31

Nabbswood Rd. ST7—2D 10
Nantwich Rd. ST7—4A 14
Napier Gdns. ST7—2C 10
Napier St. ST4—1G 29
Naples Dri. ST5—1G 27
Narvik Cres. ST6—3A 18
Nashe Dri. ST3—5J 29

Nash Peake St. ST6—2E 16
Nash St. ST5—3F 21
Nathan Clo. ST11—4J 31
Navigation Rd. ST6—6H 17
Navigation St. ST6—6G 17
Naylor St. ST6—7H 11
Neale Pl. ST2—1A 24
Neath Clo. ST3—4C 30
Neath Pl. ST3—1B 30
Nellan Cres. ST6—4B 18
Nelson Bank. ST7—5C 10
Nelson Bldgs. ST7—3C 10
Nelson Gro. ST7—2F 9
Nelson Ind. Est. ST7—3J 9
Nelson Pl. ST1—3G 23
Nelson Pl. ST5—5K 21
Nelson Rd. ST4—6B 22
Nelson St. ST4—2G 29
Nelson St. ST5—1K 21
Nephew St. ST6—5G 17
Neptune Gro. ST1—7D 18
Nethercote Pl. ST2—6C 24
Netherton Gro. ST2—4F 19
Netley Pl. ST3—1H 33
Nevada La. ST6—5K 17
Neville St. ST4—3C 28
Nevin Av. ST8—6B 6
Newark Gro. ST6—5E 10
New Av. ST11—5D 36
Newborough Clo. ST1—7D 18
New Bldgs. ST8—1A 12
Newburn Gro. ST4—7E 28
Newbury Gro. ST3—1H 33
Newcastle Enterprise Cen. ST5
—4F 21
Newcastle La. ST4—1A 28
Newcastle Rd. CW11—1A 2
Newcastle Rd. ST4—1A 28
Newcastle Rd. ST5—7K 27
Newcastle Rd. ST7—4K 9
Newcastle St. ST5—4D 20
Newcastle St. ST6—5F 17
New Century St. ST1—2E 22
Newchapel Rd. ST7—1D 10
New Clo. Av. ST11—3C 36
Newcroft Ct. ST5—1K 21
Newcrofts Wlk. ST6—6B 12
Newfield St. ST6—1F 17
Newfold Cres. ST6—4E 12
Newford Cres. ST2—4D 18
New Forest Ind. Est. ST1
—1F 23
New Hall Rd. ST3—5C 30
New Hall St. ST1—2F 23
Newhaven Gro. ST4—3E 32
New Hayes Rd. ST6—1G 17
Newhouse Ct. ST2—1A 24
Newhouse Rd. ST2—1A 24
Newington Gro. ST4—3F 33
New Inn La. CW11—1A 2
New Inn La. ST4—6C 28
New King St. ST7—4C 14
New Kingsway. ST3—3F 31
Newlands Clo. ST5—2J 27
Newlands St. ST4—5E 22
New La. ST6—3F 13
Newleigh St. ST2—4F 19
Newmill St. ST2—4E 18
Newmount Rd. ST4—2A 30
Newpool Rd. ST8—5J 5
Newpool Ter. ST8—6K 5
Newport Cotts. ST8—6K 5
Newport Gro. ST5—3A 16
Newport La. ST6—5G 17
Newport St. ST6—5G 17
New Rd. CW12—1D 4
New Rd. ST2—3E 24
New Rd. ST7—3D 14
Newshaw Wlk. ST1—2G 23
Newstead Rd. ST2—1A 24
Newstead Trading Est. ST4
—1G 33
New St. ST5—1A 22
New St. ST6—5H 17
New St. ST8—5D 6
Newton Ct. ST9—2F 25
Newton Rd. ST5—7D 16
Newton St. ST4—4B 22
Newtown. ST7—2G 11
Niall Rd. ST4—6C 28
Nicholas St. ST6—5H 17

Nicholls St. ST4—2E 28
Nile St. ST6—5J 17
Noblett Rd. ST1—6C 18
Norbury Av. ST2—4F 19
Norfolk Clo. ST5—5J 27
Norfolk Gro. ST8—2A 6
Norfolk Rd. ST7—2B 10
Norfolk St. ST1—4E 22
Normacot Grange Rd. ST3
—1F 35
Normacot Rd. ST3—4B 30
Norman Av. ST6—2H 17
Normandy Gro. ST2—3E 18
Norman Gro. ST5—4A 22
Normanton Gro. ST3—1C 30
Norris Rd. ST6—2H 17
Northam Rd. ST1—7B 18
Northcote Av. ST4—6D 22
Northcote Ct. ST5—5K 21
Northcote Pl. ST5—5K 21
Northcote St. ST4—5E 22
Northesk Pl. ST5—2H 27
Northfield Dri. ST8—1C 6
Northfleet St. ST2—3K 23
Northgate Clo. ST4—6C 28
North Pl. ST2—7F 19
North Rd. ST6—6K 17
North St. ST4—5C 22
North St. ST5—5K 21
North St. ST7—5D 4
North Ter. ST5—1J 21
North Wlk. ST3—6G 31
North W. Ter. ST6—4A 18
Northwood Clo. ST5—5A 28
Northwood Ct. ST1—2G 23
(off Ringland Clo.)
Northwood La. ST5—5K 27
Northwood Pk. Rd. ST1—1G 23
Norton Av. ST6—2J 17
Norton Cres. ST6—5B 18
Norton Dri. ST6—4B 18
Norton Hall Clo. ST6—2C 18
Norton La. ST6—1C 18
Norton St. ST2—4F 19
Norwich Pl. ST5—2K 27
Norwich Rd. ST2—4C 24
Nunn's Clo. ST3—2H 31
Nursery Av. ST9—2G 19
Nursery Clo. ST8—1A 6
Nursery La. ST9—2G 19
Nursery Rd. ST7—1A 8
(Alsager)
Nursery Rd. ST7—6A 4
(Scholar Green)
Nursery St. ST4—2D 28
Nutbrook Av. ST4—2F 29
Nyewood Av. ST3—2C 30

Oak Av. ST7—2E 8
Oakdale. ST5—4K 27
Oakdene Av. ST5—7C 16
Oakdene Clo. ST5—7C 16
Oakdene Clo. ST5—5C 36
Oakdene Gro. ST5—7C 16
Oakdene Way. ST8—4B 6
Oakham Way. ST2—4B 24
Oakhill Av. ST4—3C 28
Oakhill Hall. ST4—3C 28
Oakhurst Cres. ST3—2F 35
Oaklands Av. ST5—7E 16
Oakley Pl. ST6—4J 11
Oak Pl. ST3—5A 22
Oak Rd. ST5—4E 20
Oakshaw Gro. ST4—7E 28
Oak St. ST1—7C 18
Oak St. ST5—3A 22
Oak St. ST3—2E 2
Oaktree La. ST7—7K 9
Oak Tree Rd. ST4—2E 32
Oakville Av. ST6—3K 17
Oakwell Ct. ST3—6B 30
Oakwell Gro. ST3—6B 30
Oakwood Pl. ST5—5A 16
Oakwood Rd. ST3—6H 29
Oakwood Rd. ST7—3E 2
Oban Clo. ST5—6G 21
Oberon Clo. ST6—4B 18
Occupation St. ST5—7K 21
Odell Gro. ST6—4G 17
Odger Clo. ST3—5G 31

Ogden Rd. ST1—3F 23
Ogmore Gro. ST3—7F 31·
Ohio Gro. ST6—5K 17
Oldacres Rd. ST4—3E 32
Old Butt La. ST7—2J 9
Oldcastle Av. ST5—7C 16
Oldcott Dri. ST7—4E 10
Oldcourt St. ST6—2F 17
Oldfield Av. ST6—7B 12
Oldfield Bus. ST6—7B 12 —2J 29
Oldfield St. ST4—2K 29
Old Hall St. ST1—3F 23
Oldham St. ST1—4G 23
Oldhill Clo. ST7—7A 10
Old La. ST6—3E 12
Old Mill La. ST9—3K 19
Oldmill St. ST7—7F 23
Old Rd. ST7—2E 14
Old Rd. ST3—6C 30
Old Rd. ST15—7B 34
Old Town Rd. ST1—1F 23
Old Tramway. ST4—2J 29
Oldway Pl. ST3—2B 30
Old Wharf Pl. ST1—4H 23
Old Whieldon Rd. ST4—1F 29
Olive Gro. ST5—4K 15
Oliver Rd. ST4—7B 22
Olof Palm Gro. ST3—5B 30
Omega Way. ST4—7D 28
Ontario Gro. ST4—7D 28
Opal Rd. ST4—2H 29
Orb St. ST1—3F 23
Orchard Ct. ST7—7E 2
Orchard Cres. ST3—3K 9
Orchard Pl. ST12—7G 33
Orchard Rise. ST11—1K 35
Orchard St. ST5—1K 21
Orchard, The. ST6—4E 12
Orford Rd. ST9—5K 13
Orford St. ST5—6F 17
Orford Way. ST3—7H 29
Orgreaves Clo. ST5—5C 16
Orgreave St. ST4—7D 22
Oriel St. ST4—7D 22
Orion St. ST6—4A 18
Orkney Av. ST7—4H 11
Orlestone Pl. ST6—5J 11
Orme Rd. ST5—6G 21
Orme Rd. ST8—6B 6
Orme St. ST6—5G 17
Ormonde St. ST4—2J 29
Orpheus Gro. ST1—7D 18
Orton Rd. ST5—4H 21
Orwell Gro. ST3—2E 30
Orwell Pl. ST5—3J 27
Osborne Rd. ST4—6B 22
Oslo Gro. ST1—7D 18
Ostend Pl. ST5—7G 21
Oswald Av. ST3—2F 31
Oulton Rd. ST6—5K 11
Outclough Rd. ST8—2K 11
Oval, The. ST3—6K 29
Oval, The. ST9—2K 25
Overhouse Gro. ST6—4H 17
Overland Dri. ST6—4E 12
Oversley Rd. ST6—5J 11
Over the Hill. ST8—1E 6
Overwood Pl. ST6—5H 11
Owen Gro. ST6—5J 17
Oxford Av. ST1—6B 18
Oxford Cres. ST4—7D 22
Oxford Rd. ST3—3A 22
Oxford St. ST6—5K 11
Oxford St. ST4—6D 22
Oxhay Ct. ST5—3K 21
Oxhay View. ST5—3K 21
Ox-Hey Cres. ST8—2B 6
Ox-Hey Dri. ST8—1B 6

Pacific Rd. ST4—1D 32
Packett St. ST4—3A 30
Pack Horse La. ST6—5H 17
Paddock Cotts. ST4—2D 32
Paddock Rise. ST4—2D 32
Padlowe St. ST6—4G 17
Padston Dri. ST7—1B 8
Padstow Way. ST4—3F 33
Padworth St. ST3—4F 31
Page St. ST1—2F 23

Paisley Clo. ST2—6D 24
Paladin Av. ST3—3G 31
Palatine Dri. ST5—7K 15
Pall Mall. ST1—3F 23
Palmers Grn. ST4—6A 22
Palmerston St. ST1—4G 23
Palmerston St. ST5—1K 21
Palmerston Way. ST8—3B 6
Palmer St. ST3—3C 30
Palmers Way. ST5—6A 22
Pandora Gro. ST1—7D 18
Parade, The. ST5—5D 20
Paradise St. ST5—6J 21
Paradise St. ST6—2F 17
Paragon Av. ST5—4J 27
Paragon Rd. ST3—4C 30
Paris Av. ST5—7F 21
Parish Clo. ST7—7B 2
Park Av. ST3—2F 31
Park Av. ST5—1K 21
Park Av. ST7—4A 10
Park Av. ST9—2J 25
Park Av. W. ST5—1J 21
Park Dri. ST4—1B 32
Park Dri. ST9—2H 25
Park Dri. ST12—7F 33
Parkend. ST11—3C 36
Parker Jervis Rd. ST3—3E 30
Parker St. ST1—2F 23
Park Farm View. ST6—5F 11
Parkfield Rd. ST8—6B 30
Parkfields. ST9—5K 13
Parkfields Clo. ST5—4B 20
Parkfields Clo. ST12—7F 33
Park Hall Av. ST3—3F 31
Park Hall Cres. ST3—3F 31
Park Hall Rd. ST3—1D 30
Park Hall St. ST3—3B 30
Parkhead Cres. ST3—4F 31
Parkhead Dri. ST3—3F 31
Parkhead Gro. ST3—3F 31
Parkhouse Ind. Est. E. ST5
—4B 16
Parkhouse Ind. Est. W. ST5
—5B 16
Parkhouse Rd. E. ST5—4B 16
Parkhouse Rd. W. ST5—4A 16
Parkhouse St. ST1—4E 22
Parklands. ST7—3D 10
Parklands, The. ST8—2F 7
Park La. ST4—2J 29
Park La. ST7—1A 14
Park La. ST8—5A 6
Park La. ST9—4K 13
Parkleigh St. ST3—4B 30
Park Pl. ST4—1H 29
Park Rd. ST5—5F 27
(Butterton)
Park Rd. ST5—5C 20
(Silverdale)
Park Rd. ST6—4J 17
Park Rd. ST9—2H 25
Parkside. ST4—1E 32
Parkside Cres. ST4—4K 13
Parkside Dri. ST5—3A 22
Parkside Gro. ST5—3A 22
Parkstone Av. ST5—6K 21
Park St. ST4—1J 29
Park Ter. ST5—6A 16
Park Ter. ST6—2G 17
Park View. ST11—2K 35
Park View Ct. ST3—6A 30
Park View Rd. ST7—1C 10
Park Way. ST11—3B 36
Parkway, The. ST1—4F 23
Parkway, The. ST4—1B 32
Parkway, The. ST5—1J 27
Parkwood Av. ST4—7C 28
Parliament Row. ST1—2F 23
Parliament Sq. ST1—2F 23
Parsonage Rd. ST6—1F 17
Parton Gro. ST3—4F 31
Partridge Clo. ST3—1F 35
Patrick Pl. ST8—2K 11
Patterdale St. ST6—2J 17
Paxton St. ST1—4G 23
Paynter St. ST1—4J 29
Peacehaven Gro. ST4—3F 33
Peacock Hay Rd. ST7—1A 16
Peacock Ho. ST4—1C 32
Peacock La. ST4—7H 27

Peacock Rd. ST5—1G 21
Peacock View. ST4—5J 23
Peak Dale Av. ST6—5E 10
Peake St. ST5—3F 21
Pear Tree Clo. ST12—7G 33
Pear Tree La. ST5—5K 15
Pear Tree Rd. ST7—4F 15
Peascroft Rd. ST6—1B 18
Pebble Mill St. ST1—2C 22
Peckforton View. ST7—5C 10
Peck Mill La. ST8—3A 12
Pedley Ct. ST3—7J 29
Pedley Gro. ST6—4B 18
Peebles Grn. ST2—4B 24
Peebles Rd. ST5—4A 20
Peel Ct. ST7—2C 10
(off Attwood St.)
Peel Hollow. ST7—4A 14
Peel St. ST3—6A 30
Peel St. ST5—1K 21
Peel St. ST6—5E 16
Pegasus Gro. ST6—4B 18
Peggy's Bank. ST7—5F 15
Pegroy Gro. ST6—3B 18
Pelham St. ST1—4G 23
Pemberton Dri. ST3—3F 35
Pembridge Rd. ST3—1H 33
Pembroke Dri. ST5—7H 21
Pembroke Rd. ST2—4E 18
Penarth Gro. ST1—1F 23
Penarth Pl. ST5—7H 21
Pendine Gro. ST4—1A 30
Penfleet Av. ST3—6F 31
Pengrove Clo. ST6—4G 11
Penkhull Ct. ST4—7D 22
Penkhull New Rd. ST4—1C 28
Penkhull St. ST4—7D 22
Penk Rd. ST11—4B 36
Penkville St. ST4—2D 28
Penmark Gro. ST3—7D 30
Penmere Dri. ST5—6K 27
Penmere Dri. ST9—3F 25
Pennell St. ST2—2A 24
Pennine Way. ST5—3F 21
Pennine Way. ST8—2B 6
Pennington Clo. ST3—5H 31
Pennyfields Rd. ST7—2E 10
Pennymore Clo. ST4—7E 28
Penrhyn Av. ST6—4K 17
Penrith Clo. ST4—3F 33
Penrith Ct. ST5—1J 27
Pensford Gro. ST1—1J 23
Pentland Gro. ST5—3F 21
Penton Pl. ST3—1H 33
Pepper St. ST5—5J 21
(Keele)
Pepper St. ST5—5A 20
(Silverdale)
Perceval St. ST1—1H 23
Percival Dri. ST9—2G 19
Percy James Clo. ST7—7E 2
Percy St. ST1—2F 23
Perivale Clo. ST1—7E 18
Perkins St. ST6—5E 10
Perry Clo. ST1—3G 23
Perrymount Ct. ST4—1C 28
Persia Wlk. ST6—2F 17
Perth St. ST4—2K 29
Perthy Gro. ST4—1C 32
Petersfield Rd. ST6—5J 11
Peterson Ho. ST3—7E 30
Petrel Gro. ST3—1G 35
Pevensey Gro. ST3—1B 30
Philip La. ST9—2G 25
Philip St. ST4—1H 29
Phillipson Way. ST6—5B 18
Phoenix St. ST6—2F 17
Piccadilly. ST1—3F 23
Piccadilly Arc. ST1—2F 23
Piccadilly St. ST1—2F 17
Pickering Clo. ST3—6K 29
Pickford Pl. ST3—6E 30
Pickmere Clo. ST2—2F 19
Pickwick Pl. ST7—2K 9
Picton St. ST1—3G 23
Pidduck St. ST6—6G 17
Pierce St. ST6—2F 17
Piggott Gro. ST2—3K 23
Pikemere Rd. ST7—6B 2
Pilkington Av. ST5—1H 27
Pilsbury St. ST5—7F 17

Pilsden Pl. ST3—1H 35
Pine Clo. ST7—5K 9
Pine Ct. ST7—7E 2
Pine Ct. ST11—7J 31
Pinehurst Clo. ST5—4J 27
Pine Rd. ST4—3F 29
Pine Tree Dri. ST11—1J 35
Pinewood Cres. ST6—5G 31
Pinewood Gro. ST5—4A 16
Pinewood Gro. ST11—5B 36
Pinfold Av. ST6—1B 18
Pinhoe Pl. ST3—4D 30
Pinnox St. ST6—3G 17
Pippins, The. ST5—4K 27
Pireford Pl. ST5—4C 16
Pirehill Rd. ST5—4D 16
Pitcairn St. ST6—2G 17
Pitfield Av. ST5—3A 22
Pitgreen La. ST5—7E 16
Pit La. ST7—6J 9
Pitlea Pl. ST3—1B 30
Pitsford St. ST3—5D 30
Pitts Hill Bank. ST6—7H 11
Pitt St. E. ST6—5J 17
Pitt St. W. ST6—5J 17
Plainfield Gro. ST2—6C 24
Plaisaunce, The. ST5—1J 27
Plane Gro. ST5—4A 16
Plantation Rd. ST4—1G 33
Plant St. ST3—3B 30
Platts Av. ST9—6J 13
Pleasant St. ST6—6H 17
Plex St. ST6—2E 16
Plex, The. ST7—7D 2
Pleydell St. ST1—6D 18
Plough Croft. ST7—1A 8
Plough St. ST1—1G 23
Plover Clo. ST3—1F 35
Plumtree Gro. ST1—7D 18
Plymouth Gro. ST5—6B 16
Pochard Clo. ST6—3B 18
Podmore Av. ST7—7F 15
Podmore La. ST7—7E 14
Podmore St. ST6—6J 17
Pointon Gro. ST6—7E 12
Polperro Way. ST3—1F 35
Pool Dam. ST5—6J 21
Poole Av. ST3—2F 19
Pooles Rd. ST8—3F 7
Poolfield Av. ST5—6G 21
Poolfields Clo. ST5—6G 21
Poolside. ST3—7J 29
Pool Side. ST5—5H 21
Poolside. ST7—4G 3
Poolside Ct. ST7—7E 2
Pool St. ST4—1A 30
Pool St. ST5—6H 21
Poplar Av. ST5—3H 21
Poplar Clo. ST5—3H 21
Poplar Clo. ST11—5B 36
Poplar Ct. ST5—3H 21
Poplar Dri. ST3—5H 29
Poplar Dri. ST7—2E 8
(Alsager)
Poplar Dri. ST7—3C 10
(Kidsgrove)
Poplar Gro. ST3—6K 29
Poplar Gro. ST5—5A 22
Porlock Gro. ST4—2E 32
Porthill. ST5—7E 16
Porthill Grange. ST5—7E 16
Porthill Grn. ST5—7E 16
Porthill Rd. ST6—6F 17
Portland Clo. ST11—1J 35
Portland Dri. ST7—5A 4
Portland Dri. ST8—1B 6
Portland Dri. ST11—3C 36
Portland Gro. ST5—4J 27
Portland Pl. ST12—4J 33
Portland Rd. ST3—3A 30
Portland St. ST1—1E 22
Port St. ST6—6G 17
Port Vale St. ST6—4J 17
Port Vale St. ST6—6G 17
Post La. ST9—5K 13
Potteries Shopping Cen. ST1
—2F 23
Potteries Way. ST1—1F 23
Potters End. ST8—2K 5
Poulson St. ST4—7E 22
Pounds Gdns. ST6—1B 18

Poundsgate Clo. ST4—7E 28
Povey Pl. ST5—4D 16
Povey St. ST6—5H 17
Powderham St. ST6—4G 11
Powell St. ST1—1E 22
Power Gro. ST3—3K 29
Power Wash Trading Est. ST8
—6K 5
Powy Dri. ST7—2D 10
Prestbury Av. ST5—6J 27
Preston St. ST6—5A 18
Pretoria Rd. ST1—3D 22
Priam Clo. ST5—4D 16
Price St. ST6—4H 17
Priestley Dri. ST3—3C 30
Prime St. ST1—1H 23
Primitive St. ST6—3B 18
Primitive St. ST7—4E 4
Primrose Gro. ST5—4K 21
Primrose Hill. ST4—5D 28
Prince's Rd. ST4—6C 22
Princess Av. ST7—4D 14
Princess Clo. ST7—7K 9
Princess Dri. ST3—4F 31
Princes Sq. ST6—5F 17
Princess St. ST5—6K 21
Princess St. ST7—7K 9
Princess St. ST8—4B 6
Priorfield Clo. ST3—3A 30
Priory Pl. ST7—1D 10
Priory Rd. ST2—7F 19
Priory Rd. ST5—7H 21
Probyn Ct. ST3—5B 30
Prospect Pl. ST3—5C 30
Prospect Pl. ST4—4C 28
Prospect St. ST6—7G 17
Prospect Ter. ST5—5H 21
Providence Sq. ST1—1G 23
(off Town Rd.)
Providence St. ST1—1G 23
Puddy La. ST9—7K 13
Pump Bank. ST5—7A 20
Pump St. ST4—7D 22
Pump St. ST5—6H 21
Purbeck St. ST6—6K 17
Purser Cres. ST5—1J 21
Pyenest St. ST1—4E 22

Quabbs La. ST11—3D 36
Quadrangle, The. ST9—5K 13
Quadrant Rd. ST1—2F 23
Quail Gro. ST3—1F 35
Quarry Av. ST4—6C 22
Quarry Bank Rd. ST5—5A 20
Quarry Clo. ST9—2G 19
(Stockton Brook)
Quarry Clo. ST9—2F 25
(Werrington)
Quarry Rd. ST4—6C 22
Quarry Ter. ST7—3C 10
Queen Anne St. ST4—6E 22
Queen Elizabeth II Ct. ST4
—1G 29
Queen Mary Rd. ST4—6D 28
Queen Mary's Dri. ST12—4F 33
Queens Av. ST6—2G 17
Queensbury Rd. ST3—5C 30
Queens Clo. ST12—6J 33
Queens Ct. ST5—5K 21
Queen's Dri. ST8—5B 6
Queens Gdns. ST7—6K 9
Queensmead Rd. ST3—1E 34
Queens Pde. ST5—5J 21
(off Merrial St.)
Queen's Pk. Av. ST3—6A 30
Queen's Rd. ST4—6C 22
Queen's Row. ST12—6J 33
Queen's Ter. ST1—2H 23
Queen St. ST5—6A 16
(Chesterton)
Queen St. ST5—5K 21
(Newcastle)
Queen St. ST5—7D 16
(Porthill)
Queen St. ST6—5H 17
(Audley)
Queen St. ST7—2C 10
(Kidsgrove)
Queen's Wlk. ST3—3G 31

Queensway. ST4
—4C 22 to 5C 28
Queensway. ST5—1J 27
Queensway. ST7—6B 2
Queensway Ind. Est. ST6
—5E 16
Quinton Gro. ST5—2J 21
Quinton Wlk. ST6—3B 18

Race Course. ST5—5D 20
Racecourse Rd. ST4—3D 28
Rachel Gro. ST4—1A 30
Radford Rd. ST4—5C 22
Radley Way. ST9—3G 25
Radstone Rise. ST5—4J 27
Raglan St. ST4—1G 29
Raglan Wlk. ST4—1G 29
(off Raglan St.)
Railton Av. ST3—6K 29
Railway Cotts. ST4—4F 29
Railway Cotts. ST11—7E 36
Railway Ct. ST9—5K 13
Railway Pas. ST3—3B 30
Railway Rd. ST3—5D 30
Railway St. ST6—3G 17
Railway Ter. ST3—4B 30
Railway Ter. ST11—1K 35
Rainford Clo. ST3—3H 11
Rainham Gro. ST6—4J 11
Ralph Dri. ST1—5C 18
Ramage Gro. ST3—6C 30
Ramsay Clo. ST12—3H 33
Ramsey Rd. ST5—4H 21
Ramsey St. ST4—2F 29
Ramshaw Gro. ST3—3E 30
Randel La. ST6—4D 10
Ranelagh St. ST1—3F 23
Rangemore Ter. ST5—3A 22
Ransome Pl. ST3—3E 30
Ranworth Clo. ST5—5J 27
Rathbone Av. ST5—3A 22
Rathbone St. ST6—2G 17
Rattigan Dri. ST3—3E 30
Ratton St. ST2—2G 23
Ravenscliffe. ST5—6E 16
(off First Av.)
Ravenscliffe Rd. ST7—4C 10
Ravens Clo. ST7—2E 14
Raven's La. ST7—2F 15
Ravenswood Clo. ST5—4H 27
Rawlins St. ST1—1H 23
Rayleigh Way. ST2—5C 24
Raymond Av. ST1—6B 18
Raymond St. ST1—4F 23
Reading Way. ST2—4C 24
Rebecca St. ST4—6E 22
Recorder Gro. ST6—6K 11
Recreation Rd. ST3—5D 30
Rectory Pas. ST1—4E 22
Rectory Rd. ST1—4E 22
Rectory St. ST1—4E 22
Rectory View. ST7—6K 9
Red Bank. ST3—6B 30
Redbridge Clo. ST4—6C 28
Redcar Rd. ST4—1D 32
Red Hall La. ST7—7C 14
Redheath Clo. ST5—4B 20
Red Heath Cotts. ST5—4A 20
Redhills Rd. ST2—4E 18
Red Ho. Cres. ST3—4K 29
Redlands Dri. ST2—3C 24
Red La. ST7—2G 9
Red Lion Clo. ST7—5K 9
Red Lion Pas. ST1—3E 22
Red Lion Sq. ST5—6A 16
Redman Gro. ST6—6A 18
Redmine Clo. ST7—3C 10
Redwing Dri. ST8—3C 6
Redwood Pl. ST3—6E 30
Reedbed Clo. ST6—2A 18
Reedham Way. ST2—4C 24
Reeves Av. ST5—2J 21
Reeves Av. ST6—2J 17
Refinery St. ST6—5J 17
Regency Clo. ST7—7K 9
Regent Av. ST6—2H 17
Regent Ct. ST5—7D 16
Regent Rd. ST1—4F 23
Regent St. ST4—2C 28
Reginald St. ST6—5J 17

Regina St. ST6—3B 18
Registry St. ST4—6E 22
Reid St. ST6—5G 17
Remer St. ST6—7K 17
Renard Way. ST3—1G 35
Renfrew Clo. ST5—7G 21
Renfrew Pl. ST4—6D 28
Renown Clo. ST2—5J 23
Repington Rd. ST1—5C 18
Repton Dri. ST5—2G 27
Reservoir Rd. ST3—5D 30
Reynolds Av. ST5—7A 16
Reynolds Rd. ST6—2J 17
Rhodes Ct. ST5—6E 16
Rhodes St. ST1—7B 18
Rhondda Av. ST6—6A 18
Rialto Pl. ST6—2F 17
Ribble Clo. ST5—3J 27
Ribble Dri. ST8—2C 6
Ricardo St. ST3—6A 30
Riceyman Rd. ST5—4D 16
Richards Av. ST6—2H 17
Richardson Pl. ST6—6K 11
Richmond Av. ST1—6B 18
Richmond Gro. ST5—3B 22
Richmond Rd. ST4—6C 28
Richmond St. ST4—6D 22
Richmond Ter. ST1—4E 22
Ridding Bank. ST4—7J 27
Ridge Clo. ST12—7F 33
Ridge Cres. ST3—2E 34
Ridgefields Rd. ST8—2F 7
Ridgehouse Dri. ST1—2D 22
Ridge Rd. ST6—6F 11
Ridgmont Rd. ST5—3G 27
Ridgway Dri. ST11—1J 35
Ridgway Pl. ST5—7F 17
Ridgway Rd. ST4 & ST1—5F 23
Ridley St. ST4—2F 29
Ridley Wlk. ST4—2F 29
Rigby Rd. ST7—1D 10
Riley Av. ST6—3K 17
Riley St. N. ST6—5G 17
Riley St. S. ST6—5H 17
Rileys Way. ST7—3F 15
Rill St. ST4—3A 30
Ringland Clo. ST1—2G 23
Ripon Av. ST5—6A 16
Ripon Rd. ST3—7J 29
Riseley Rd. ST4—6A 22
Rists Ind. Est. ST5—2G 21
Rists Rd. ST5—2G 21
Riverdale Dri. ST6—4G 11
Riverhead Clo. ST6—7D 12
Riverside Rd. ST4—4B 28
Riversmead. ST5—3J 27
Rivington Cres. ST6—6J 11
Rixdale Clo. ST1—1F 23
Robert Heath St. ST6—3A 18
Roberts Av. ST5—4H 21
Roberts Clo. ST7—7F 15
Robertson Dri. ST5—3G 21
Robertson Sq. ST4—3B 28
Robert St. ST6—1F 17
Robertville Rd. ST2—3A 24
Robin Croft. ST6—5H 17
Robin Hill Gro. ST4—2A 30
Robinson Av. ST6—5B 18
Robinson Ct. ST3—7J 29
Robinson Rd. ST4—7C 28
Robson St. ST1—3E 22
Rochester Rd. ST3—2A 30
Rochford Way. ST2—5C 24
Rockfield Av. ST2—4H 19
Rock Ho. Dri. ST12—7G 33
Rockhouse La. ST7—4J 9
Rocklands. ST5—6E 16
Rockside. ST7—5E 4
Rocks, The. ST6—4F 13
Rode Ho. Clo. ST7—4F 3
Rode, The. ST7—7D 2
Rodgers St. ST6—4E 10
Rodmore St. ST6—6J 17
Roebuck Shopping Cen. ST5
—6J 21
Roebuck St. ST4—6F 23
Roe La. ST5—3H 27
Rogate Clo. ST4—1A 30
Rogers Av. ST5—3G 21
Rogerstone Av. ST4—1B 28

Rolfe Clo. ST4—5D 28
Roman Dri. ST5—1E 20
Romer Side. ST2—6B 24
Romford Pl. ST3—1G 35
Romney Av. ST5—7A 16
Romsey Clo. ST2—6C 24
Ronald St. ST3—5B 30
(in two parts)
Ronaldsway Dri. ST5—4H 21
Ronald Wlk. ST3—5B 30
Ronson Av. ST4—3B 28
Rookery Av. ST3—6K 29
Rookery La. ST4—4C 28
Rookery Rd. ST7—1E 10
Rookery, The. ST5—5D 20
Rope St. ST4—5A 22
Roseacre. ST5—7G 21
Roseacre Gro. ST3—2E 34
Roseacre La. ST11—5A 36
Roseberry St. ST6—7H 11
Rosebery Clo. ST8—3C 6
Rose Cotts. ST9—3K 13
Rosehill Clo. ST2—4F 19
Roseland Cres. ST2—4F 19
Rosemary Pl. ST1—6C 18
Rosemary Pl. ST5—5F 21
Rosendale Av. ST5—7B 16
Roseneath Pl. ST2—4F 19
Rosery, The. ST4—1B 32
Rose St. ST1—1H 23
Rose Tree Av. ST4—5B 28
Rosevale Ct. ST5—5A 16
Rosevale Rd. ST5—5A 16
Rosevale St. ST2—4F 19
Rosevean Clo. ST1—1F 23
Rosewood Av. ST9—1G 19
Rossall Av. ST5—2G 27
Ross Clo. ST3—3F 31
Rossett Gro. ST6—4H 11
Rosslyn Rd. ST3—5B 30
Rosy Bank. ST9—2G 19
Rothbury St. ST3—4B 30
Rother Wlk. ST6—1J 17
Rothesay Av. ST5—7G 21
Rothesay Ct. ST3—5C 30
Rothesay Ct. ST5—7G 21
Rothesay Rd. ST3—5C 30
Rothley Grn. ST3—7J 29
Rothsay Av. ST1—5B 18
Rothwell St. ST4—1C 28
Rotterdam. ST5—5G 21
Rotterdam Rd. ST5—2G 17
Roughcote La. ST11—1H 31
Roughwood La. CW11—2A 2
Roundfields. ST9—2G 19
Roundway. ST3—5G 29
Roundwell St. ST6—2F 17
Rowanburn Clo. ST3—2C 30
Rowan Clo. ST7—4C 10
Rowan Clo. ST8—3F 7
Rowan Gro. ST3—4G 29
Rowan Pl. ST5—5A 16
Rowhurst Clo. ST5—6K 15
Rowhurst Clo. Ind. Est. ST5
—6J 15
Rowhurst Pl. ST6—7A 12
Rowland St. ST3—6A 30
Rowley Av. ST5—6B 16
Rownall Pl. ST3—5F 31
Rownall Rd. ST3—5F 31
Rownall Rd. ST9—2J 25
Roxburghe Av. ST3—5C 30
Royal Overhouse Pottery. ST6
(off New St.) —5H 17
Royal St. ST4—2K 29
Royce Av. ST6—6K 5
Royden Av. ST1—2J 23
Roylance St. ST6—2F 17
Royston Wlk. ST3—4B 30
Royville Pl. ST6—5B 18
Rubian St. ST4—1J 29
Rudyard Gro. ST5—2K 21
Rudyard Rd. ST8—2F 7
Rugby Clo. ST5—3G 27
Rugby Dri. ST3—6A 30
Runnymede Clo. ST2—3A 24
Rupert St. ST3—3A 6
Rushcliffe Dri. ST3—1F 35
Rushmoor Gro. ST3—1G 35
Rushton. ST5—3G 27
Rushton Clo. ST6—5F 13

Rushton Gro. ST6—6J 17
Rushton Rd. ST6—6J 17
Rushton Way. ST11—3B 36
Rusper Clo. ST1—7D 18
Russell Av. ST7—6D 2
Russell Gro. ST9—2G 25
Russell Pl. ST6—6F 11
Russell Rd. ST6—6F 11
Russell St. ST3—6A 30
Russell St. ST5—1K 21
Rustington St. ST3—4D 30
Ruston Av. ST6—6K 11
Rutherford Av. ST5—4J 27
Rutherford Pl. ST4—7B 22
Ruthin Rd. ST2—4B 24
Rutland Pl. ST5—3K 27
Rutland Rd. ST3—3B 30
Rutland Rd. ST7—2C 10
Rutland St. ST1—1E 22
Ruxley Cl. ST2—3K 23
Ruxley Rd. ST2—3K 23
Rydal Way. ST5—3J 27
Rydal Way. ST7—6C 2
Ryder Rd. ST3—7E 30
Rye Bank. ST5—5J 21
Rye Bank Cres. ST5—5K 21
Ryebrook Gro. ST6—6H 11
Rye Clo. ST7—1B 8
Ryecroft. ST5—5J 21
Ryecroft Rd. ST6—2C 18
Rye Hills. ST7—4E 14
Rylestone Clo. ST3—1G 35

Sackville St. ST4—4A 22
Saffron Clo. ST3—2F 35
St Aidan's St. ST6—1F 17
St Andrews Cres. ST1—6B 18
St Andrew's Dri. ST5—6G 21
St Andrews Dri. ST7—1E 10
St Andrews Gdns. ST7—2E 8
St Andrews Sq. ST4—7D 22
St Anne's Vale. ST4—3F 13
St Ann St. ST1—2G 23
St Ann Wlk. ST1—2G 23
(off St Ann St.)
St Anthony's Dri. ST5—7G 21
St Bartholomews Clo. ST6
—1C 18
St Bernard Pl. ST2—1K 23
St Bernard's Rd. ST5—4G 21
St Chads Rd. ST6—2G 17
St Chad's Ter. ST5—3K 15
St Christopher Av. ST4—1B 28
St Clair St. ST3—5B 30
St Edmund's Av. ST5—6F 17
St Georges Av. ST6—1J 17
St Georges Av. ST9—6J 13
St Georges Av. N. ST5—1J 21
St Georges Av. S. ST5—1J 21
St Georges Av. W. ST5—1J 21
St Georges Cres. ST4—6D 28
St George's Rd. ST5—6H 21
St Giles Rd. ST5—4G 21
St Gregorys Rd. ST3—4K 29
St Helier Clo. ST5—4G 27
St James Pl. ST4—6D 28
St James St. ST1—3E 22
St John's Av. ST4—3B 28
St John's Av. ST5—2K 21
St John's Pl. ST5—4G 21
St John's Rd. ST8—5A 6
St John's Sq. ST6—5H 17
St John St. ST1—1G 23
St Johns Wood. ST7—3D 8
St Joseph St. ST6—5F 11
St Lucy's Dri. ST5—6E 16
St Luke's Clo. ST5—4C 20
St Lukes Ct. ST1—3G 23
(off Perry Clo.)
St Luke St. ST1—3G 23
St Margaret's Ct. ST5—1A 22
St Margaret's Dri. ST1—5C 18
St Margarets Gro. ST3—4H 29
St Mark's Clo. ST1—4E 22
St Mark's St. ST1—4E 22
St Martins La. ST3—4B 30
St Martin's Rd. ST5—6G 21
St Martin's Rd. ST7—6A 10
St Mary's Clo. ST7—6C 2
St Mary's Dri. ST5—6H 21

St Mary's Rd. ST3—2C 30
St Mary's Rd. ST5—1A 22
St Matthew St. ST4—1J 29
St Michael's Ho. ST6—6H 11
St Michael's Rd. ST5—3J 21
St Michael's Rd. ST6—7H 11
St Nicholas Av. ST6—2C 18
St Patrick's Dri. ST5—6G 21
St Pauls Ct. ST3—5J 29
St Pauls Pl. ST6—5G 17
(off St Pauls St.)
St Paul's Rd. ST5—5H 21
St Pauls St. ST6—5G 17
St Peter's Wlk. ST6—7J 17
St Saviour's St. ST7—3K 9
St Thomas Pl. ST4—1C 28
St Thomas St. ST7—4G 5
St Vincent Pl. ST5—4F 21
Salcombe Pl. ST1—6B 18
Salem St. ST1—3C 22
Salisbury Av. ST1—4F 23
Salisbury St. ST6—2G 17
Salkeld Pl. ST6—7K 11
Salop Gro. ST5—3K 27
Salop Pl. ST7—1C 10
Saltdean Clo. ST3—5C 30
Salters Clo. ST9—3G 25
Salters La. ST9 & ST3—3G 25
Sampson St. ST1—2E 22
Samuel St. ST7—3H 11
Sancton Grn. ST6—6G 17
Sandbach Rd. ST6—6K 17
Sandbach Rd. ST7—5D 2
(Lawton Heath End)
Sandbach Rd. ST7—2D 2
(Rode Heath)
Sandbach Rd. N. ST7—7C 2
Sandbach Rd. S. ST7—1D 8
Sandcrest Pl. ST3—6D 30
Sandcrest Wlk. ST3—6E 30
Sandford St. ST3—2B 30
Sandford St. ST5—5A 16
Sandgate St. ST3—4C 30
Sandhurst Av. ST3—6E 30
Sandhurst Clo. ST5—1K 21
Sandhurst Pl. ST3—7E 30
Sandiway Pl. ST1—7C 18
Sandon Av. ST5—2H 27
Sandon Ct. ST3—1E 34
Sandon Old Rd. ST3—1E 34
Sandon Rd. ST3—1E 34
Sandon St. ST1—3D 22
Sandown Pl. ST2—3G 19
Sandra Clo. ST6—3J 17
Sandringham Cres. ST4
—6D 28
Sandsdown Clo. ST8—2A 6
Sandside Rd. ST7—1B 8
Sands La. ST6—1E 12
Sands Rd. ST7—5G 5
Sandwell Pl. ST3—7D 30
Sandwick Cres. ST1—7D 18
Sandwood Cres. ST3—2B 30
Sandyfield Rd. ST1—1H 23
Sandy Hill. ST9—2H 25
Sandylands Cres. ST7—6F 3
Sandy La. ST2—3G 19
Sandy La. ST5—4K 21
Sandy La. ST6—4F 13
Sandy Rd. ST5—7F 11
Sandy Rd. ST8—1A 6
Sangster La. ST6—3B 18
Sant St. ST6—5G 17
Saplings, The. ST5—4K 27
Saracen Way. ST3—6F 31
Sargeant Av. ST6—6J 11
Sark Clo. ST5—3F 27
Sark Pl. ST3—1C 30
Saturn Rd. ST6—4A 18
Saunders Rd. ST5—2J 21
Saverley Grn. Rd. ST11—7K 35
Sawyer Dri. ST8—2A 6
Scarlett St. ST5—6J 21
Scarratt Clo. ST11—3C 36
Scarratt St. ST11—4C 36
Sceptre St. ST1—3F 23
School Clo. ST7—4G 15
School La. ST3—7J 29
School La. ST8—1F 7
School La. ST11—4J 31
School Rd. ST2—1K 23

Stoke 51

School Rd. ST9—3K 19
School St. ST4—4B 28
School St. ST5—7B 16
(Chesterton)
School St. ST5—5K 21
(Newcastle)
Scot Hay Rd. ST5—3A 20
Scot Hay Rd. ST7—1A 20
Scotia Ho. ST6—6H 11
Scotia Rd. ST6—2G 17
Scott Lidgett Ind. Est. ST6
—6F 17
Scott Lidgett Rd. ST6—6F 17
Scott Rd. ST6—7H 11
Scott St. ST5—5K 21
Scragg St. ST7—4H 11
Scrimshaw Dri. ST6—2A 18
Scrivener Rd. ST4—5C 22
Seabridge La. ST5—3F 27
Seabridge Rd. ST5—7H 21
Seaford St. ST4—5E 22
Seagrave Pl. ST5—1H 27
Seagrave St. ST5—5K 21
Seaton Clo. ST3—7D 30
Sebring Av. ST3—7D 30
Second Av. ST2—3C 24
Second Av. ST5—6E 16
Second Av. ST7—3A 10
Sedbergh Clo. ST5—3G 27
Seddon Ct. ST1—2G 23
(off Linfield Rd.)
Seddon Rd. ST3—7E 30
Sedgley Wlk. ST3—3B 30
Seedfields Rd. ST3—4H 29
Sefton Av. ST1—6C 18
Sefton Rd. ST3—5D 30
Sefton St. ST1—3D 22
Selbourne Dri. ST6—5H 11
Selby Clo. ST5—2H 27
Selby St. ST3—2G 31
Selby Wlk. ST3—1H 33
Selwood Clo. ST3—6C 30
Selworthy Rd. ST6—7E 12
Selwyn St. ST4—1E 28
Settle Gro. ST3—7F 31
Seven Arches Way. ST4—7F 23
Sevenoaks Gro. ST3—2G 35
Severn Clo. ST8—3C 6
Severn Dri. ST5—4J 27
Severn St. ST1—1E 22
Seymour St. ST1—3H 23
Shady Gro. ST7—7D 2
Shaftesbury Av. ST6—3J 19
Shakespeare Clo. ST7—4C 10
Shaldon Av. ST9—1G 19
Shannon Dri. ST6—5E 10
Shardlow Clo. ST4—1K 29
Shawport Av. ST5—5C 16
Shaw St. ST1—1D 22
Shaw St. ST5—5J 21
Shaw St. ST8—4A 6
Sheaf Pas. ST3—4B 30
Sheaf St. ST1—4E 22
Shearer St. ST1—4E 22
Shefford Rd. ST5—4G 27
Shelburne St. ST4—2D 28
Sheldon Gro. ST5—7B 16
Sheldrake Gro. ST4—1A 30
Shelford Rd. ST6—6F 11
Shelley Clo. ST7—4C 10
Shelley Rd. ST2—7F 19
Shelton New Rd. ST4—5A 22
Shelton Old Rd. ST4—6D 22
Shemilt Cres. ST6—2A 18
Shendon Ct. ST5—6C 16
Shenfield Grn. ST2—4C 24
Shenton St. ST3—2C 30
Shepherd St. ST8—4A 6
Shepley Gro. ST3—1H 33
Sheppard St. ST4—1D 28
Sherborne Clo. ST3—1H 33
Sherborne Dri. ST5—2H 27
Sheridan Gdns. ST3—5J 29
Sheringham Pl. ST5—2A 22
Sherratt St. ST6—2A 18
Sherwin Rd. ST6—2H 17
Sherwood Rd. ST3—1E 34
Shetland Rd. ST3—4J 29
Shillingford Dri. ST4—7E 28
Shilton Clo. ST4—2C 28
Shinwell Gro. ST3—7F 31

Ship Pl. ST6—3A 18
Shirebrook Clo. ST3—1H 33
Shirley Av. ST9—2G 25
Shirley Rd. ST1—4F 23
Shirley St. ST6—5F 17
Short Bambury St. ST3—1C 30
Short St. ST3—4B 30
Shorwell Gro. ST6—4G 11
Shotsfield Pl. ST2—4E 18
Shotsfield St. ST2—4E 18
Showan Av. ST5—3A 22
Shraleybrook Rd. ST7—5A 14
Shrewsbury Dri. ST5—3A 16
Shugborough Clo. ST9—4F 25
Sidcot Pl. ST1—6B 18
Sideway Rd. ST4—3E 28
Sidings Pl. ST3—3A 30
Sidmouth Av. ST5—5K 21
Sillitoe Pl. ST4—1D 28
Silsden Gro. ST3—5H 31
Silver Clo. ST8—3A 6
Silverdale. ST5—4D 20
Silverdale Rd. ST5—5E 20
(Newcastle)
Silverdale Rd. ST5—1K 21
(Wolstanton)
Silverdale St. ST5—3F 21
Silver Ridge. ST12—7F 33
Silverstone Cres. ST6—4G 11
Silver St. ST6—1C 18
Silverton Clo. ST5—5C 16
Silverwood. ST7—3D 10
Simonburn Av. ST4—1B 28
Simon Pl. ST4—5E 22
Simpson St. ST1—4G 23
Simpson St. ST5—1J 21
Sinclair Av. ST7—1B 8
Siskin Pl. ST3—1G 35
Sitwell Gro. ST3—3C 30
Skellern Av. ST6—2A 18
Skellern St. ST7—2K 9
Skipacre Av. ST6—4B 18
Skye Clo. ST3—4D 30
Slacken La. ST7—2K 9
Staldburn gro. ST1—1J 23
Slaney St. ST5—7K 21
Slapton Clo. ST2—5J 23
Slater St. ST6—6G 17
Slater St. ST8—4A 6
Slippery La. ST3—1G 35
Sloane Way. ST4—1A 30
Smallwood Clo. ST5—4K 15
Smallwood Gro. ST1—7D 18
Smith Child St. ST6—1F 17
Smith Clo. ST7—7B 2
Smithfield Ct. ST1—4F 23
Smithpool Rd. ST4—2G 29
Smiths Pas. ST4—2K 29
Smith St. ST3—3B 30
Smithyfield Rd. ST6—1B 18
Smithy Gro. CW11—1A 2
Smithy La. ST3—4B 30
Smithy La. ST8—1B 6
Sneyd Av. ST5—7G 21
Sneyd Cres. ST5—7G 21
Sneyd Hill. ST6—5K 17
Sneyd Pl. ST6—6E 10
Sneyd St. ST6—7K 17
Sneyd Ter. ST5—4C 20
Sneyd Trading Est. ST6
(in two parts)—5K 17 & 4A 18
Snowden Way. ST3—5G 31
(in two parts)
Snow Hill. ST1—4E 22
Soames Cres. ST3—1A 30
Solway Gro. ST3—3D 30
Somerley Rd. ST1—7D 18
Somerset Av. ST7—2B 10
Somerset Rd. ST2—2H 23
Somerton Rd. ST9—3F 25
Somerton Way. ST3—2C 30
Somerville Av. ST5—3A 22
Sorrel Clo. ST2—3K 23
Souldern Way. ST3—3C 30
Southall Way. ST2—5K 23
Southampton St. ST1—1G 23
Southborough Cres. ST6
—1A 18
South Clo. ST7—7A 2
Southern Ct. ST4—7D 22
Southern Way. ST6—4B 18

Southgate Av. ST4—2F 33
Southlands. ST5—1K 21
Southlands Av. ST3—6A 30
Southlowe Av. ST9—2K 25
Southlowe Rd. ST9—2K 25
South Pl. ST6—6B 12
South Rd. ST2—1A 24
South St. ST6—6B 12
South St. ST7—5D 4
South Ter. ST4—2D 28
South Ter. ST5—1K 21
South View. ST3—4E 34
South View. ST8—3A 6
South Wlk. ST3—6G 31
South Wolfe St. ST4—7E 22
Spalding Pl. ST2—6D 24
Sparch Av. ST5—2K 21
Sparch Gro. ST5—2K 21
Sparch Hollow. ST5—2K 21
Spark St. ST4—7D 22
Spark Ter. ST4—7D 22
Sparrow St. ST6—3B 18
Sparrow Ter. ST5—7D 16
Spa St. ST6—6A 18
Speakman St. ST3—5C 30
Spedding Rd. ST4—6H 23
Spedding Way. ST8—3C 6
Speedwall St. ST3—2B 30
Speedwell Rd. ST5—4B 16
Spencer Av. ST9—6J 13
Spencer Clo. ST7—7A 2
Spencer Pl. ST5—7A 16
Spencer Rd. ST4—6F 23
Spencroft Rd. ST5—1G 21
Spens St. ST6—5H 17
Sperry Clo. ST3—1G 35
Spey Dri. ST7—2E 10
Spinney Clo. ST9—4J 13
Spinney, The. ST5—5K 27
Spinney, The. ST7—7A 4
Spire Clo. ST6—2C 18
Spode Gro. ST5—4J 27
Spode St. ST4—2E 28
Spoutfield Rd. ST4—5C 22
Spout Hollow. ST6—6K 9
Spout La. ST2—4G 19
Spragg Ho. La. ST6—2C 18
Spratslade Dri. ST3—5A 30
Spring Bank. ST7—3C 4
Springbank Av. ST9—6J 13
Spring Clo. ST7—3E 2
Spring Cres. ST6—5G 13
Springcroft. ST11—5A 36
Springfield Cres. ST3—5A 30
Springfield Dri. ST11—3B 36
Springfield Rd. ST8—4B 6
Springfields. ST11—2K 35
Springfields Rd. ST4—1B 28
Spring Garden Rd. ST3—5A 30
Spring Garden Ter. ST3—5A 30
Springhead Clo. ST7—6K 9
Springpool. ST5—1D 26
Spring Rd. ST3—5D 30
Springs Bank. ST9—3K 19
Springside Pl. ST3—1H 33
Spring St. ST4—5A 22
Springwood Rd. ST5—5J 15
Sprink Bank Rd. ST6—7J 11
Sprinkwood Gro. ST3—4F 31
Sproston Rd. ST6—1B 18
Spruce Gro. ST7—4F 3
Spur St. ST1—4G 23
Square, The. ST3—5G 31
Square, The. ST5—1J 27
Squires View. ST4—7F 23
Squirrel Hayes Av. ST8—5C 6
Squirrels, The. ST5—4K 27
Stadmorslow La. ST7
—7H 5 to 2J 11
Stafford Av. ST5—2K 27
Stafford Cres. ST5—3K 27
Stafford La. ST1—2F 23
Stafford St. ST1—2F 23
Stallington Clo. ST11—4J 35
Stallington Gdns. ST11—5A 36
Stallington Rd. ST3 & ST11
—6G 35
Stamer St. ST4—1E 28
Standard Av. ST4—1G 29
Standersfoot Pl. ST6—6K 11

Stanfield Rd. ST6—4J 17
Stanfield St. ST3—1C 30
Stanhope St. ST1—4E 22
Stanier St. ST4—2H 29
Stanier St. ST5—5H 21
Stanley Bank. ST9—7K 13
Stanley Ct. ST7—7C 2
Stanley Gro. ST2—3F 19
Stanley Gro. ST5—4A 22
Stanley Moss La. ST9—7J 13
Stanley Moss Rd. ST9—7J 13
Stanley Rd. ST4—6B 22
Stanley Rd. ST5—4A 22
Stanley Rd. ST8—1A 6
Stanley Rd. ST9—1H 19
Stanley St. ST6—1G 17
Stanley St. ST8—3A 6
Stansgate St. ST1—1E 22
Stansmore Rd. ST3—5G 31
Stanton Clo. ST5—4G 21
Stanton Rd. ST3—6F 31
Stanway Av. ST6—6A 18
Stanways La. ST8—1F 7
Stapleton Cres. ST3—6K 29
Star & Garter Rd. ST3—6D 30
Starwood Rd. ST3—7D 30
Statham St. ST1—3E 22
Station Bri. Rd. ST4—2H 29
Station Cres. ST6—3B 18
Station Gro. ST2—4E 18
Station Rd. ST4—6E 22
Station Rd. ST5—6A 20
(Keele)
Station Rd. ST5—4C 20
(Silverdale)
Station Rd. ST7—1C 8
(Alsager)
Station Rd. ST7—6D 14
(Halmer End)
Station Rd. ST7—3B 10
(Kidsgrove)
Station Rd. ST7—3D 4
(Mow Cop)
Station Rd. ST7—2G 11
(Newchapel)
Station Rd. ST7 & CW12—4A 4
(Scholar Green)
Station Rd. ST8—2A 6
Station Rd. ST9—5K 13
Station Rd. ST12—7G 33
Station St. ST6—6F 17
Station View. ST6—6F 17
Station Wlks. ST5—5J 21
Station Wlks. ST7—6D 14
Staveley Clo. ST2—3K 23
Staveley Pl. ST5—5B 20
Stedman St. ST1—1G 23
Steele Av. ST6—3K 17
Steel St. ST4—6B 22
Stellar St. ST6—4A 18
Stephens Way. ST7—3F 15
Sterndale Dri. ST4—1A 30
Sterndale Dri. ST5—4J 27
Stevenson Rd. ST2—2K 23
Steventon Pl. ST6—5H 17
Stewart Ct. ST2—5C 24
Stewart St. ST4—1G 29
Stile Clo. ST8—4A 6
Stockfield Rd. ST3—1E 34
Stockwood Rd. ST5—3G 23
Stoke Old Rd. ST4—5A 22
Stokesay Gro. ST6—6J 17
Stone Bank. Rd. ST7—4D 10
Stone Chair La. ST7—4A 4
Stonehaven Gro. ST1—4G 23
Stonehouse La. ST6—3B 12
Stonehouse Rd. ST9—3G 25
Stoneleigh Rd. ST6—7J 11
Stone Rd. ST3—5D 34
Stone Rd. ST4 & ST12
—5C 28 to 7D 32
Stone St. ST4—7D 22
(in two parts)
Stonewall Pl. ST5—4E 20
Stonewall Pl. Ind. Est. ST5
—4E 20
Stonewood Clo. ST4—4B 28
Stoneycroft. ST2—3F 19
Stoneyfields. ST8—3F 7

Stoneyfields Av. ST2—3F 19
Stoneyfields Ct. ST5—4A 22
Stoney La. ST9—5J 13
Stoney Vs. ST2—3G 19
Stonor St. ST6—7J 17
Stormont Clo. ST6—3A 18
Stowell Grn. ST4—6B 22
Stowford Gro. ST4—7D 28
Stradbroke Dri. ST3—6K 29
Strand Clo. ST2—4K 23
Strand Pas. ST3—3A 30
(off Strand, The.)
Strand, The. ST3—4A 30
Stranraer Clo. ST3—3G 31
Stratford Av. ST5—3A 22
Stratford Clo. ST6—4D 18
Stratford Clo. ST11—3B 36
Stratheden Rd. ST6—3K 17
Street La. CW11 & ST7—1E 2
Stretton Rd. ST5—4A 20
Stringer St. ST8—3A 6
Stroma Clo. ST6—6H 17
Stross Av. ST6—7H 11
Stroud Clo. ST3—1G 35
Stuart Av. ST4—1D 32
Stuart Av. ST11—5D 36
Stuart Gro. ST5—2K 21
Stuart Rd. ST1—4G 23
Stubbsfield Rd. ST5—7K 21
Stubbs Ga. ST5—6K 21
Stubbs La. ST1—3G 23
Stubbs St. ST5—6J 21
Stubbs St. ST6—5G 17
Stubbs Wlks. ST5—6K 21
Sturgess St. ST4—1D 28
Sudbourne Clo. ST4—4G 11
Sudbury Pl. ST5—5J 27
Sudgrove Pl. ST3—1G 35
Sudlow St. ST6—6K 17
Suffolk Clo. ST5—3A 28
Summerbank Rd. ST6—1F 17
Summerfield. ST7—3D 10
Summer Hill Dri. ST5—4K 15
Summer Row. ST5—5A 30
Summer St. ST4—2D 28
Summerville Rd. ST4—4B 28
Sunbury Clo. ST4—2F 33
Sundorne Pl. ST2—4A 24
Sunningdale Clo. ST6—2K 17
Sunningdale Gro. ST5—5K 15
Sunnycroft Av. ST3—6K 29
Sunnyfield Oval. ST2—4G 19
Sunny Hollow. ST5—3K 21
Sunnyside. ST7—7A 2
Sunnyside Av. ST6—2H 17
Sunridge Clo. ST2—3F 19
Sun St. ST1—4D 22
Surrey Rd. ST7—2C 10
Surtees Gro. ST4—2A 30
Sussex Dri. ST7—2B 10
Sutherland Av. ST3—6A 30
Sutherland Cres. ST11—1K 35
Sutherland Dri. ST5—2G 27
Sutherland Pl. ST3—5C 30
Sutherland Rd. ST3—4B 30
Sutherland Rd. ST12—6D 32
Sutherland St. ST4—1F 29
Sutton Dri. ST4—3C 28
Sutton Pl. ST6—7K 11
Sutton St. ST5—7A 16
Swaffham Way. ST2—4C 24
Swainsley Clo. ST6—6J 17
Swallow Clo. ST3—1F 35
Swallow Clo. ST7—2C 10
Swallowmore View. ST7—4J 9
Swallow Wlk. ST4—4C 6
Swanage Clo. ST3—1G 35
Swan Bank. ST7—5K 9
Swan Clo. ST7—4K 9
Swanland Gro. ST3—3C 30
Swan La. ST4—4B 28
Swan Sq. ST5—5H 17
Swan St. ST4—6D 22
Swanton Pl. ST4—1C 32
Swaythling Gro. ST2—5C 24
Swettenham Clo. ST7—1C 8
Swift Clo. ST7—2D 10
Swift Dri. ST8—3C 6
Swift Pl. ST3—2E 30
Swinburne Clo. ST3—5J 29
Swingle Hill Rd. ST3—4J 29

Swithin Dri. ST4—1A 30
Sycamore Av. ST7—2E 8
(Alsager)
Sycamore Av. ST7—4F 3
(Rode Heath)
Sycamore Clo. ST3—3F 35
Sycamore Clo. ST7—4A 10
Sycamore Clo. ST8—1C 6
Sycamore Gro. ST3—4G 29
Sycamore Gro. ST5—3A 22
Sydenham Pl. ST2—6C 24
Sydney St. ST5—4A 22
Sylvan Gro. ST4—4B 28
Sylvester St. ST6—5J 17
Sytch Rd. ST6—5F 13

Tabor St. ST4—2J 29
Talbot St. ST1—4G 23
Talke Rd. ST5—2A 16
Talke Rd. ST7—1E 8
(Alsager)
Talke Rd. ST7 & ST5—2K 15
(Talke Pits)
Tallis Gro. ST1—1J 23
Talsarn Gro. ST4—2F 22
Tamar Rd. ST7—2D 10
Tame Clo. ST8—2B 6
Tame Wlk. ST3—3F 31
Tanners Rd. ST2—6F 19
Tansy Clo. ST2—3K 23
Target Clo. ST7—6A 10
Tarleton Rd. ST1—2H 23
Tarporley Gro. ST4—2B 28
Tarragon Dri. ST3—2F 35
Tarvin Gro. ST6—6H 11
Tasman Sq. ST1—1H 23
Tatton Clo. ST7—1C 8
Tatton St. ST3—5B 30
Taunton Pl. ST5—6B 16
Taunton Way. ST2—4C 24
Taurus Gro. ST6—6H 11
Tavistock Cres. ST5—2H 27
Tavistock Pl. ST4—5B 22
Tawney Clo. ST7—2D 10
Tawney Cres. ST3—4G 31
Tay Clo. ST8—2C 6
Taylor Av. ST5—2K 21
Taylor Rd. ST2—7F 19
Taylor St. ST5—2K 21
Taylor St. ST6—5E 10
Taynton Clo. ST6—4J 11
Teal View. ST6—3B 18
Telford Clo. ST7—4A 10
Telford Way. ST6—1J 17
Tellwright Gro. ST5—6C 16
Tellwright St. ST6—4J 17
Telford St. ST4—1G 29
Templeton Av. ST2—6B 24
Tenbury Grn. ST2—5B 24
Tenby Gro. ST5—6B 16
Tennant Pl. ST5—6D 16
Tennyson Av. ST7—4C 10
Tennyson Gdns. ST3—5J 29
Terence Wlk. ST8—2K 11
Tern Av. ST7—2E 10
Tern Clo. ST8—3C 6
Terrington Dri. ST5—5J 27
Terry Clo. ST3—4G 31
Terson Way. ST3—3E 30
Tewkesbury Gro. ST2—2K 23
Tewson Grn. ST6—6A 18
Thackeray Dri. ST3—5K 29
Thames Dri. ST8—2B 6
Thames Rd. ST5—4H 27
Thanet Gro. ST3—4K 29
Thatchems Grn. ST3—1H 33
Thatcher Gro. ST8—3K 5
Thelma Av. ST6—5F 13
Theodore Rd. ST2—3A 24
Theresa Clo. ST5—5D 28
Third Av. ST2—2C 24
Third Av. ST7—3A 10
Thirlmere Gro. ST3—4D 30
Thirlmere Pl. ST2—2J 27
Thirsk Pl. ST5—4B 20
Thistleberry Av. ST5—7G 21

Thistleberry Ho. ST5—6G 21
Thistley Hough. ST4—1C 28
Thomas Av. ST5—2H 21
Thomas Clo. ST7—7E 2
Thomas St. ST7—3H 11
(Packmoor)
Thomas St. ST7—4K 9
(Talke)
Thomas St. ST8—2A 6
Thompstone Av. ST5—3G 21
Thornburrow Dri. ST4—7B 22
Thorncliff Gro. ST1—1J 23
Thorndyke St. ST1—4E 22
Thorne Pl. ST3—4G 31
Thorneycroft Av. ST6—3K 17
Thornham Clo. ST5—5J 27
Thornham Grn. ST2—5B 24
Thornhill Rd. ST2—6D 24
Thornley Rd. ST6—2H 17
Thornton Rd. ST4—6F 23
Thorpe Grn. ST3—1J 33
Thurlwood Dri. ST6—3D 18
Thursfield St. ST6—1B 18
Thursfield Wlk. ST6—7B 12
Thurston Way. ST2—6B 24
Thyme Gro. ST3—2G 35
Tibb St. ST7—3F 15
Tiber Dri. ST5—1E 20
Tidebrook Pl. ST6—5G 11
Tideswell Rd. ST3—2B 30
Tierney St. ST1—1G 23
Tilbrook Clo. ST2—6B 24
Tilehurst Pl. ST3—6H 29
Tilery La. ST3—6G 29
Tilewright Clo. ST7—2D 10
Tillet Grn. ST3—4G 31
Till Wlk. ST3—1C 30
Tilson Av. ST4—7C 22
Tilstone Clo. ST7—4C 10
Timble Clo. ST2—6B 24
Times Sq. ST3—3A 30
Timmis St. ST1—3D 22
Timor Gro. ST4—7E 28
Timothy Clo. ST3—1B 30
Tintagel Pl. ST2—6B 24
Tintern Pl. ST5—6B 16
Tintern St. ST1—3H 23
Tipping Av. ST3—6G 31
Tirley St. ST4—2H 29
Tissington Pl. ST3—1H 35
Tittensor Rd. ST5—2K 27
Tittensor Rd. ST12—7E 32
Titterton St. ST4—1F 29
Tiverton Rd. ST2—5B 24
Toft End Rd. ST5—4D 16
Tolkien Way. ST4—6D 22
Toll Bar Rd. ST9—2J 25
Tollgate Clo. ST7—4J 9
Tollgate Ct. ST3—7J 29
Tomfields. ST7—5F 15
Tomlinson St. ST6—5F 17
Tompkin Rd. ST9—7K 13
Tonbridge Av. ST6—1K 17
Toney Pl. ST2—3J 23
Tongue La. ST6—4C 12
Tontine Sq. ST1—2F 23
Tontines Shopping Ct., The.
(off Tontine St.) ST1—2F 23
Tontine St. ST1—2F 23
Topham Pl. ST2—3J 23
Top Heath's Row. ST6—4F 13
Top Rd. ST8—2J 7
Top Station Rd. ST7—4E 4
Torres Wlk. ST1—1H 23
Torridan Clo. ST4—2F 33
Tor St. ST1—6B 18
Torville Dri. ST8—3C 6
Tower Clo. ST8—5K 5
Tower Hill Rd. ST7 & ST8—3G 5
Tower Sq. ST6—2F 17
Townend. ST11—7K 35
Townfield Clo. ST7—2K 9
Town Rd. ST1—2F 23
Townsend La. ST7—3G 3
Townsend Pl. ST2—3A 24
Trade St. ST4—7E 22
Trafalgar Rd. ST4—6B 22
Trafalgar St. ST1—1F 23
Transport La. ST3—4A 30
Tranter Rd. ST2—7F 19

Travers Ct. ST4—1G 29
Travers St. ST6—6G 17
Tregaron Ct. ST2—3F 25
Tregenna Clo. ST3—1F 35
Tregew Pl. ST5—4E 20
Tregowan Clo. ST6—2K 17
Trentfields Rd. ST2—3F 19
Trent Gro. ST5—4H 27
Trent Gro. ST8—5B 6
Trentham Gdns. Clo. ST4
—1C 32
Trentham Gro. ST5—2K 21
Trentham M. ST4—1D 32
Trentham Rd. ST4 & ST3
—1F 33 to 4B 30
Trentham Rd. ST5—7D 26
Trentley Dri. ST8—3F 7
Trentley Rd. ST4—1C 32
Trentmill Rd. ST1—4H 23
Trent Rd. ST11—3B 36
Trentside Rd. ST6—7E 12
Trent St. ST2—3J 23
Trent Ter. ST6—7E 12
Trent Valley Rd. ST4—3C 28
Trent Wlk. ST1—4G 23
Trentway Clo. ST2—3K 23
Trevor Dri. ST11—4J 31
Trimley Way. ST2—4A 24
Triner Pl. ST6—1C 18
Tring Clo. ST2—6B 24
Trinity Cl. ST5—5A 16
Trinity Pl. ST2—2A 24
Trinity St. ST1—2F 23
Triton Wlk. ST6—4B 18
Troutdale Clo. ST4—7A 24
Trowbridge Cres. ST2—4B 24
Trubshawe Cross. ST6—5F 17
Trubshawe St. ST6—5F 17
Trubshaw Pl. ST7—1D 10
Truro Pl. ST2—4A 24
Tudor Clo. ST4—1D 28
Tudor Ct. ST5—7D 16
Tudor Ct. ST11—7A 36
Tudor Gro. ST5—2K 21
Tudor Hollow. ST11—7K 35
Tudors, The. ST6—1G 17
Tulip Gro. ST5—4K 21
Tulley Pl. ST2—3K 23
Tulsa Clo. ST2—5K 23
Tunbridge Dri. ST4—4A 20
Tunnel Ter. ST6—1D 16
Tunnicliffe Clo. ST3—4D 30
Tunstall Greenway. ST6
—1G 17
Tunstall Rd. ST8—6A 6
Turin Dri. ST5—1F 27
Turnberry Dri. ST4—7D 28
Turner Av. ST7—4G 15
Turner Cres. ST5—7A 16
Turner St. ST1—1G 23
Turnhill Gro. ST5—6B 16
Turnhurst Rd. ST7 & ST6
—3H 11
Turnlea Clo. ST8—5K 5
Turnock St. ST2—2B 24
Tuscan Ho. ST3—5A 30
Tuscan Clo. ST3—3B 30
Tuscan Way. ST5—7K 15
Tutbury Clo. ST3—3C 30
Tweed Gro. ST5—3H 27
Tweed St. ST4—3H 29
Twemlow St. ST1—3D 22
Twigg St. ST7—2A 4
Twyning Grn. ST3—1J 33
Tyler Gro. ST5—6J 17
Tyndall Pl. ST4—7B 22
Tyneham Gro. ST2—3E 18
Tyne Way. ST5—3H 27
Tynwald Grange. ST5—4H 21
Tyrell Gro. ST1—5D 18
Tyson St. ST2—6C 24

Ubberley Grn. ST2—4B 24
Ubberley Rd. ST2—4A 24
Uffington Pde. ST2—5B 24
Ufton Clo. ST3—2J 33
Ullswater Av. ST6—5G 17
Ulster Ter. ST4—2D 28
Ulverston Rd. ST3—1J 33
Umberleigh Rd. ST3—1H 33

Under the Hill. ST8—2E 6
Underwood Rd. ST5—5A 20
Unicorn Pl. ST6—7H 11
Union Ct. ST1—1F 23
Union St. ST1—1F 23
Unity Av. ST1—6B 18
Unity Ho. ST1—3F 23
Unity Way. ST7—4K 9
Unwin St. ST6—2K 17 & 2A 18
(in two parts)
Uplands Av. ST6—6H 11
Uplands Av. ST9—3F 25
Uplands Croft. ST9—2F 25
Uplands Dri. ST9—3F 25
Uplands Rd. ST2—6F 19
Uplands, The. ST5—4K 21
Uplands, The. ST8—1C 6
Up. Belgrave Rd. ST3—6C 30
Upper Cres. ST4—6B 22
Up. Cross St. ST3—3B 30
Up. Furlong St. ST4—1G 29
Up. Hillchurch St. ST1—2G 23
Up. Huntbach St. ST1—2G 23
Up. Market Sq. ST1—2F 23
Up. Marsh. ST5—3A 22
Up. Normacot Rd. ST3—5C 30
Urmston Pl. ST3—1J 33
Utterby Side. ST2—6B 24
Uttoxeter Rd. ST3 & ST11
—4B 30 to 6E 36

Valentine Rd. ST7—3C 10
Vale Pl. ST1—1E 22
Vale Pleasant. ST5—4D 20
Valerian Way. ST3—2F 35
Vale St. ST4—7E 22
Vale St. ST5—5A 16
(Chesterton)
Vale St. ST5—4C 20
(Silverdale)
Vale View. ST5—6F 17
Valley Clo. ST7—1A 8
Valley Rd. ST3—4G 31
Vauxhall St. ST3—4B 30
Velvet St. ST6—5H 17
Venice Ct. ST5—7F 21
Venn St. ST1—4H 23
Ventnor Gro. ST3—2J 33
Venton Clo. ST6—1C 18
Verney Way. ST3—1J 33
Vernon Av. ST7—3C 14
Vernon Clo. ST7—3D 14
Vernon Rd. ST4—6E 22
Vessey Ter. ST5—6K 21
Vicarage Cres. ST5—7K 21
Vicarage Cres. ST11—4J 31
Vicarage Cres. ST12—7D 32
Vicarage La. ST4—3B 28
Vicarage La. ST12—6H 33
Vicarage Rd. ST4—6C 22
Vichy Clo. ST5—7F 21
Vickers Rd. ST6—7J 11
Victoria Av. ST1—4F 23
Victoria Av. ST7—6E 14
(Halmer End)
Victoria Av. ST7—2B 10
(Kidsgrove)
Victoria Clo. ST5—4D 20
Victoria Cotts. ST3—5D 30
Victoria Ct. ST5—3K 21
Victoria Ct. ST7—2C 10
(off Attwood St.)
Victoria Pk. Rd. ST6—2G 17
Victoria Pl. ST4—1H 29
Victoria Pl. ST5—6A 16
(Chesterton)
Victoria Pl. ST5—1A 22
(Wolstanton)
Victoria Rd. ST1 & ST4—5G 23
Victoria Rd. ST5—6K 21
Victoria Row. ST8—7A 6
Victoria Sq. ST1—3E 22
Victoria St. ST4—4A 22
Victoria St. ST5—6A 16
(Chesterton)
Victoria St. ST5—6K 21
(Newcastle)
Victoria St. ST5—4D 20
(Silverdale)
Vienna Pl. ST5—1G 27

Views, The. ST7—2G 11
Viggars Pl. ST5—4G 21
Villa Clo. ST8—5A 6
Villas, The. ST4—2D 28
Villa St. ST4—2D 28
Villiers St. ST3—6A 30
Vincent St. ST1—1H 23
Vine Bank Rd. ST7—2C 10
Vinebank St. ST4—1D 28
Vine Row. ST4—1D 28
Viscount Wlk. ST3—1E 34
Vivian Rd. ST4—1J 29
Vowchurch Way. ST2—5B 24

Wade Av. ST5—7F 17
Wadebridge Rd. ST2—5A 24
Wade St. ST6—4K 17
Wadham St. ST4—7D 22
Wain Av. ST5—6G 21
Wain Av. ST6—7C 12
Wain Dri. ST4—1B 28
Wain St. ST6—4H 17
Wainwood Rise. ST4—2C 28
Wainwright Wlk. ST1—2G 23
(off Wellington St.)
Wakefield Rd. ST4—3C 28
Walcot Gro. ST2—5K 23
Walker Rd. ST6—1H 17
Walkersgreen Rd. ST5—3K 15
Walkers La. ST1—1H 3
Walker St. ST6—3F 17
Walklate Av. ST5—3A 22
Walley Dri. ST6—6F 11
Walley Pl. ST6—6J 17
Walley's Dri. ST5—4A 22
Walley St. ST6—6J 17
Walley St. ST3—3A 6
Wallis Pl. ST2—1A 24
Wallis St. ST4—1J 29
Wallis Way. ST2—3E 18
Wallmires La. ST9—5J 25
Walmer Pl. ST3—2A 30
Walney Gro. ST1—1F 23
Walnut Av. ST4—5B 28
Walnut Gro. ST5—5K 15
Walpole St. ST3—2C 30
Walsingham Gdns. ST5—5J 27
Walton Cres. ST4—2F 29
Walton Gro. ST7—4J 9
Walton Pl. ST5—7B 16
Walton Rd. ST4—4C 28
Walton Way. ST7—4J 9
Warburton St. ST6—6J 17
Wardle La. ST2—4G 19
Wardle St. ST6—2G 17
Ward Pl. ST6—7K 11
Warminster Pl. ST3—4K 29
Warmson Clo. ST3—1B 30
Warner St. ST1—3F 23
Warren Pl. ST5—5C 30
Warren Rd. ST6—6K 11
Warren St. ST3—5C 30
Warrilowheath Rd. ST5—4J 15
Warrington Rd. ST4—5G 23
Warrington St. ST1—1J 29
Warsill Gro. ST3—3C 30
Warwick Av. ST3—6E 30
Warwick Av. ST5—3K 27
Warwick Clo. ST7—1C 10
Warwick Gro. ST5—3B 22
Warwick St. ST1—3D 22
Warwick St. ST5—6A 16
Warwick St. ST8—4A 6
Washerwall La. ST9—2F 25
Washerwall St. ST2—6C 24
Washington Clo. ST8—1A 6
Washington St. ST6—3G 17
Watchfield Clo. ST3—6E 30
Waterbeck Gro. ST4—3F 33
Waterdale Gro. ST3—4D 30
Waterfall Cotts. ST9—6H 13
Watergate St. ST6—2F 17
Waterhead Rd. ST3—6E 30
Waterloo Gro. ST7—2C 10
Waterloo Rd. ST6 & ST1—5J 17
Waterloo St. ST1—3G 23
Waterside Dri. ST3—1H 33
Water St. ST4—2D 28
Water St. ST5—5K 21
(Newcastle)

Water St. ST5—3K 15
(Red Street)
Watery La. ST3—6C 30
Watford St. ST4—6F 23
Watkin St. ST4—2G 29
Watlands Av. ST5—1K 21
Watlands Rd. ST7—3E 14
Watlands View. ST5—1J 21
Watson Rd. ST4—3C 28
Watson St. ST4—6C 22
Waveney Cr. ST5—3J 27
Waveney Gro. ST5—3J 27
Waveney Wlk. N. ST6—1J 17
Waveney Wlk. S. ST6—1J 17
Waverley Pl. ST5—2J 27
Waverton Rd. ST2—7D 24
Wavertree Av. ST7—4A 4
Wayfield Gro. ST4—6A 22
Wayside. ST7—2F 9
Wayside Av. ST5—2K 21
Wayte St. ST1—1E 22
Weaver Clo. ST7—1A 8
Weaver Clo. ST8—2B 6
Weaver Pl. ST5—3J 27
Weaver St. ST1—2F 23
Webberley La. ST3—5B 30
Webb St. ST3—4G 31
Webster Av. ST3—2D 30
Webster St. ST5—6K 21
Wedgewood Av. ST7—4F 15
Wedgewood Ct. ST1—3D 22
Wedgwood Av. ST5—7G 21
Wedgwood Dri. ST12—5F 33
Wedgwood La. ST8—1A 6
Wedgwood La. ST12—4H 33
Wedgwood Pl. ST6—5H 17
Wedgwood Rd. ST4—1J 29
Wedgwood Rd. ST7—5K 9
Wedgwood St. ST5—2K 15
(Chesterton)
Wedgwood St. ST5—1A 22
(Wolstanton)
Wedgwood St. ST6—5H 17
Weetman Clo. ST6—5E 10
Weighton Gro. ST2—5D 24
Weir Gro. ST7—2D 10
Welbeck Pl. ST2—1B 24
Welby St. ST4—2G 29
Welch St. ST4—7E 22
Weldon Av. ST3—3G 31
Welland Gro. ST5—4H 27
Wellbury Clo. ST4—3F 33
Weller St. ST4—6C 22
Wellesley St. ST1—1E 22
Wellfield Rd. ST2—4A 24
Wellington Ct. ST1—2G 23
Wellington Rd. ST1—2G 23
Wellington Rd. ST7—2C 10
Wellington St. ST1—3G 23
Wellington St. ST5—1K 21
Wellington Ter. ST1—3G 23
Well La. ST7—1C 8
Well La. ST8—1A 6
Wells Clo. ST8—1A 6
Well St. ST1—3G 23
Well St. ST5—6K 21
Well St. ST7—4F 5
Well St. ST8—3A 6
Well St. ST11—3B 36
Welsh Row. ST7—4G 5
Wem Gro. ST5—3A 16
Wendling Clo. ST2—5C 24
Wendover Gro. ST7—5B 4
Wendy Clo. ST2—5A 24
Wenger Cres. ST4—1C 32
Wenham Dri. ST3—1G 35
Wenlock Clo. ST5—3A 16
Wenlock Clo. ST6—4K 11
Wentworth Dri. ST7—1E 10
Wentworth Gro. ST1—5D 18
Werburgh Dri. ST4—1C 32
Wereton Rd. ST7—4D 14
Werrington Rd. ST2—3K 23
Wesker Pl. ST3—3E 30
Wesley Av. ST7—7D 2
Wesley Gdns. ST7—2C 10
Wesley Pl. ST5—6G 21
Wesley Pl. ST7—6D 14
Wesley St. ST6—2F 17
Wesley St. ST7—4G 15
(Bignall End)

Wesley St. ST7—4K 9
(Talke)
Wesley St. ST11—4B 36
Wessex Dri. ST4—7D 28
Westacre. ST1—3J 23
West Av. ST4—6C 22
West Av. ST5—4A 22
West Av. ST7—4J 9
West Bank. ST4—1D 28
Westbourne Dri. ST6—7G 11
W. Brampton. ST5—5J 21
Westbury Cen., The. ST5
—5J 27
Westbury Clo. ST1—1J 23
Westbury Rd. ST5—4J 27
Westcliffe Av. ST5—4H 27
West Cres. ST1—5C 18
Westerby Dri. ST9—3F 25
Westerham Clo. ST4—1C 32
Westfield Av. ST3—3C 14
Westfield Rd. ST2—3A 24
Westfield Rd. ST7—4E 4
West Gro. ST7—7E 2
Westhead Wlk. ST3—1E 22
Westlands. ST7—3F 15
Westlands Av. ST5—7G 21
Westland St. ST4—7D 22
Westmarsh Gro. ST6—1J 17
Westmill St. ST1—4G 23
Westminster Pl. ST4—6D 28
Westmorland Av. ST7—5B 10
Westmorland Clo. ST6—4J 11
Weston Clo. ST2—3F 25
Weston Clo. ST5—3G 21
Weston Coyney Rd. ST3
—4D 30
Weston Dri. ST3—3F 31
Westonfields Dri. ST3—4D 30
Weston Rd. ST3—6F 31
Weston St. ST3—1C 30
Westonview Av. ST3—2C 30
West Pde. ST4—2F 29
Westport Greenway. ST6
(off Davenport St.) —4F 17
Westport Greenway. ST6
(off Scotia Rd.) —3H 17
Westport Rd. ST6—4G 17
W. Precinct. ST1—3F 23
Westsprink Cres. ST3—5D 30
West St. ST3—2G 31
West St. ST5—6K 21
(Newcastle)
West St. ST5—6F 17
(Porthill)
West St. ST5—5C 20
(Silverdale)
West St. ST7—5D 4
West St. ST8—4A 6
West Ter. ST6—6K 11
West Ter. ST7—3C 10
West View. ST3—4E 34
West View. ST5—1J 21
Westwood Ct. ST1—2G 23
Westwood Rd. ST3—5F 31
Westwood Rd. ST5—7F 17
Wetherby Clo. ST5—6A 16
Wetherby Rd. ST4—1E 32
Wetley Av. ST9—2K 25
Weybourne Av. ST2—2F 19
Whalley Av. ST4—1B 28
Wharfedale Wlk. ST3—4K 29
Wharf Pl. ST4—7F 23
Wharf Rd. ST8—3A 6
Wharf St. ST5—5A 22
Whatmore St. ST6—4A 18
Wheatfields. ST6—2A 18
Wheatley Bank Cotts. ST2
—3K 23
Wheatly Av. ST4—1B 28
Wheelock Clo. ST7—1A 8
Wheelock Way. ST7—2D 10
Whetstone Rd. ST8—1A 6
Whieldon Cres. ST4—2G 29
Whieldon Rd. ST4—1F 29
Whimple Side. ST2—5A 24
Whitaker Rd. ST3—4H 29
Whitbread Dri. ST3—2A 30
Whitchurch Gro. ST5—3A 16
Whitcliffe Pl. ST3—4J 29
Whitcombe Rd. ST3—5F 31
Whitebeam Clo. ST5—4K 15

Whitehall Av. ST7—2B 10
Whitehall Rd. ST7—2B 10
Whitehaven Dri. ST1—1E 22
Whitehead Rd. ST6—7K 11
Whitehill Rd. ST7—2C 10
Whitehill Ter. ST7—2D 10
Whitehouse Rd. ST2—1K 23
Whitehouse Rd. ST3—3J 21
Whitehouse Rd. N. ST5—2J 21
Whiteridge Rd. ST7—2C 10
Whitesands Gro. ST3—2G 35
Whitestone Rd. ST3—2G 35
Whitethorn Av. ST12—7G 33
Whitethorn Way. ST5—4A 16
Whitfield Av. ST5—6H 21
Whitfield Greenway. ST6
              —1H 17
Whitfield Rd. ST6—5B 12
Whitfield Vs. ST6—6B 12
Whitley Rd. ST6—6B 12
Whitmore Av. ST9—2G 25
Whitmore Rd. ST4—7A 28
Whitmore Rd. ST5—7J 27
  (Butterton)
Whitmore Rd. ST5—1A 26
  (Keele)
Whitmore Rd. ST5
  (Whitmore) —7C 26 to 1H 27
Whitmore St. ST1—3E 22
Whitridge Gro. ST2—6C 24
Whittle Rd. ST3—7G 31
Whygate Gro. ST1—7D 18
Widecombe Rd. ST1—7D 18
Wigmore Pl. ST3—1B 30
Wignall Rd. ST6—6F 11
Wilbraham's Wlk. ST7—3D 14
Wilbrahams Way. ST7—7D 2
Wilding Rd. ST6—6B 12
Wileman Pl. ST4—1H 29
Wileman St. ST4—1H 29
Wilfred Pl. ST4—6C 22
Wilkinson St. ST6—3F 17
Wilks St. ST6—1G 17
Willatt Pl. ST2—4E 18
Willdale Gro. ST1—1J 23
Willeton St. ST2—3K 23
Willfield La. ST6—5F 13
William Av. ST3—7H 31
William Av. ST8—4B 6
William Birch Ct. ST2—5K 23
William Birch Rd. ST2—5K 23
William Clo. ST11—4C 36
William Clowes St. ST6—5H 17
William Fiske Ct. ST4—3C 28
William Rd. ST7—2C 10
William Rushton Rd. ST6
              —3B 18
Williamson Av. ST6—6B 12
Williamson St. ST6—3G 17
William St. ST4—1H 29
William Ter. ST6—6K 11
Willotts Hill Rd. ST5—4K 15
Willoughby St. ST6—5F 11
Willow Clo. ST5—4K 15
Willow Clo. ST7—5C 10
Willow Ct. ST7—7E 2
Willowdale Av. ST4—2F 29
Willow Gro. ST3—5H 29
Willow La. ST3—5F 35
Willowood Gro. ST3—7H 31

Willow Pl. ST8—2F 7
Willow Row. ST3—4A 30
Willows Dri. ST3—4F 35
Willow Tree Gro. ST7—4F 3
Willow Way. ST11—3B 36
Wilmer Cres. ST7—5D 4
Wilmot Clo. ST5—3G 21
Wilmot Dri. ST5—3G 21
Wilmot Gro. ST3—1B 30
Wilson Rd. ST4—6C 28
Wilson St. ST5—5J 21
Wilson St. ST6—3K 17
Wilson Way. ST6—5E 10
Wilton Av. ST9—2K 25
Wilton St. ST5—4H 21
Wiltshire Gro. ST5—3K 27
Wimberry Dri. ST5—4K 15
Wimborne Av. ST3—1J 33
Winchester Av. ST2—4B 24
Winchester Dri. ST5—3G 27
Windermere Rd. ST5—3J 27
Windermere St. ST1—1E 22
Windmill Av. ST7—4C 10
Windmill Clo. ST3—4E 34
Windmill Hill. ST3—4E 34
Windmill St. ST1—2G 23
Windmill View. ST9—2H 25
Windrush Clo. ST4—3F 33
Windsmoor St. ST4—2E 28
Windsor Av. ST3—5C 30
Windsor Dri. ST7—7A 2
Windsor Rd. ST4—6D 28
Windsor St. ST5—5K 21
Wingate Wlk. ST3—1J 33
Winghay Clo. ST5—5E 16
Winghay Pl. ST6—7K 11
Winghouse La. ST12—7C 32
Wingrove Av. ST3—6C 30
Winifred Gdns. ST3—7H 29
Winifred St. ST1—1E 22
Winnipeg St. ST4—7E 28
Winpenny Rd. ST5—5B 16
Winsford Av. ST3—5D 30
Winslow Grn. ST2—5B 24
Winston Av. ST7—7C 2
Winston Pl. ST2—3K 23
Winston Ter. ST5—7E 16
Winterbourne Gro. ST3—4D 30
Winterfield La. ST3—6G 25
Winterside Clo. ST5—4K 15
Wintonfield St. ST4—7F 23
Winton Sq. ST4—6E 22
Wise St. ST3—6B 30
Witchford Cres. ST3—1J 33
Witham Way. ST8—2C 6
Withies Rd. ST4—3B 28
Withington Rd. ST6—5J 11
Withnell Grn. ST6—6J 11
  (off Meiklejohn Pl.)
Withystakes Rd. ST9—2J 25
Witney Wlk. ST3—1J 33
Woburn Clo. ST4—3F 33
Wolfe St. ST4—1E 28
Wolseley Rd. ST4—3C 28
Wolseley Rd. ST5—1J 21
Wolstanton Retail Pk. ST5
              —1A 22
Wolstanton Rd. ST5—7B 16
Wolstern Rd. ST3—2C 30

Woodall St. ST1—1E 22
Woodbank St. ST6—5H 17
Woodberry Av. ST4—2B 28
Woodberry Clo. ST4—2C 28
Woodbridge Rd. ST5—5J 27
Woodcock La. ST7—5E 4
Wood Cotts. ST9—5J 13
Woodcroft. ST7—4G 15
Wood Dri. ST7—1A 8
Woodend St. ST4—1J 29
Woodgate Av. ST7—6G 3
Woodgate St. ST3—6F 31
Woodhall Pl. ST5—4A 20
Woodhall Rd. ST7—1E 10
Woodhead Rd. ST2—6F 19
Woodhouse La. ST6—6C 12
Woodhouse La. ST8—1C 6
Woodhouse St. ST4—1E 28
Wooding Dean Clo. ST3—2C 30
Woodkirk Clo. ST6—6J 11
Woodland Av. ST5—1K 21
Woodland Av. ST6—1D 18
Woodland Ct. ST7—6D 2
Woodland Gro. ST3—4F 35
Woodland Rd. ST7—3E 2
Woodlands. ST1—1C 22
Woodlands Av. ST7—2K 9
Woodlands Gro. ST3—4F 35
Woodlands La. ST11—6C 36
Woodlands Rd. ST4—3B 28
Woodlands, The. ST4—3B 28
Woodland St. ST6—2G 17
Woodland St. ST8—4B 6
Woodman St. ST2—4F 19
Woodpark La. ST3—1C 34
Wood Pl. ST3—5G 31
Woodruff Clo. ST7—3H 11
Woodshutts St. ST7—3K 9
Woodside. ST7—7A 4
Woodside Av. ST6—6F 13
Woodside Av. ST7—7E 2
  (Alsager)
Woodside Av. ST7—3C 10
  (Kidsgrove)
Woodside Cres. ST5—5K 27
Woodside Dri. ST3—4F 35
Woodside Pl. ST2—4F 19
Woodside Vs. ST3—3C 30
Woodstock Clo. ST5—3K 21
Woodstock Rd. ST6—5C 10
Woodstock St. ST6—4E 10
Woodstone Av. ST9—6J 13
Wood St. ST3—3B 30
Wood St. ST7—2E 14
  (Bignall End)
Wood St. ST7—4E 4
  (Mow Cop)
Wood Ter. ST1—4E 22
Wood, The. ST3—5H 31
Woodvale Cres. ST9—4J 13
Wood View. ST7—4G 15
Woodville Pl. ST3—5F 31
Woodville Rd. ST3—5F 31
Woodville Ter. ST3—5G 31
Woodward St. ST1—7B 18
Woolaston Dri. ST7—1D 8
Wooliscroft Rd. ST2—3A 24
Woolliscroft Av. ST5—3A 22
Woolrich St. ST6—6G 17

Worcester Clo. ST7—5K 9
Worcester Pl. ST2—4C 24
Wordsworth Way. ST7—7D 2
Worth Clo. ST3—3C 30
Worthing Pl. ST3—4A 30
Wraggs La. ST8—2F 7
Wrenbury Cres. ST2—5A 24
Wren Clo. ST8—3C 6
Wrexham Clo. ST8—2B 6
Wright Av. ST5—6B 16
Wrighton Clo. ST4—6J 23
Wright St. ST7—3K 9
Wroxham Way. ST5—5J 27
Wulstan Dri. ST5—3K 21
Wulstan Rd. ST6—7J 17
Wyatt St. ST6—5E 10
Wycliffe St. ST6—5H 17
Wye Rd. ST5—3H 27
Wymondley Gro. ST4—2E 32
Wynbank Clo. ST7—5E 14
Wyndham Rd. ST3—1J 33
Wynford Pl. ST3—2A 24
Wynstay Av. ST9—3F 25
Wynstay Ct. ST5—6K 27

Yale St. ST6—6G 17
Yardley Pl. ST3—2J 33
Yardley St. ST6—7D 12
Yardley Wlk. ST3—2J 33
Yarmouth Wlk. ST3—2C 30
Yarnbrook Gro. ST6—2B 18
Yarnfield Clo. ST3—5F 31
Yarrow Pl. ST3—2F 35
Yateley Clo. ST2—4A 24
Yates St. ST1—3E 22
Yaxley Ct. ST5—5J 27
Yaxley Pl. ST3—2J 33
Yeaman St. ST4—1E 28
Yeldham Pl. ST3—2J 33
Yeovil Pl. ST3—2J 33
Yew Pl. ST5—5K 15
Yew Tree Av. ST3—5H 29
Yew Tree Clo. ST2—4H 19
Yew Tree Ct. ST7—2E 8
Yew Tree La. CW12—1D 4
Yew Tree Ter. ST7—4C 10
York Av. ST11—7K 35
York Clo. ST7—5K 9
York Clo. ST8—1B 6
York Clo. ST11—3C 36
York Pl. ST5—5J 21
York Rd. ST3—4G 31
York St. ST1—1E 22
York St. ST5—6K 21
Youlgreave Av. ST2—4A 24
Youlton Pl. ST2—4A 24
Younger St. ST4—1G 29
Young St. ST6—6H 11
Yoxall Av. ST4—6C 22

Zamenhof Gro. ST6—4A 18
Zennor Gro. ST2—4A 24
Zetland Pl. ST3—2J 33
Zetland Wlk. ST3—2J 33
Zion St. ST6—5J 17
Zodiac Dri. ST6—6H 11

Printed by THE **KPC** GROUP London and Ashford, Kent